OBA'S STORY

OBA'S STORY

Rastafari, Purification and Power

by

George D. Colman

Africa World Press, Inc.

P.O. Box 1892
Trenton, NJ 08607

P.O. Box 48
Asmara, ERITREA

Africa World Press, Inc.

First Printing 2005

Book design: Sam Saverance
Cover design: Roger Dormann
Cover Photo by Author

Library of Congress Cataloging-in-Publication Data

Colman, George D.
Oba's story : Rastafari, purification, and power / by George D. Colman.
p. cm.
Includes bibliographical references (p. 167).
ISBN 1-59221-321-9 (cloth) -- ISBN 1-59221-322-7 (pbk.)
1. Chatoyer, Ras Oba, 1948- 2. Rastafarians--Saint Vincent and the Grenadines--Biography. I. Title.

BL2532.R37C65 2005
299.6'76'092--dc22

2005016438

To

Dafina and Michele

Acknowledgements

My gratitude to Oba and Dafina is, of course, large and lasting. Over several years, Oba gave himself fully and enthusiastically to the work of remembering his life, sorting through his memories, answering endless questions, and stitching together a cohesive story. Dafina, his wife and mother of their six children, welcomed us into their home, offered friendship and shared her very different story.

I have been grateful for the incisive, stimulating thoughts of my wife, Michele Gibbs, for long years now. A fine critic, she read and improved each early and later version of the text with her judgements and suggestions.

Conversations with members of the Nyahbinghi Order regarding the roles of Rasta men and Rasta women were especially valuable to me. My sincere thanks to Sister I-Deka, Sister I-Land, Sister Azziza Miyazya, and I-Man-I for their openness to my questions and their thoughtful responses.

I was fortunate that in my desire to place Oba's life and work in the context of a broader social and political history I could be guided by a range of scholars whose work on

Caribbean history and specifically on Rastafarians is cited in the footnotes following the text.

My sincere thanks go to Kassahun Checole, the founder of Africa World Press, for his strong evaluation of the book and his decision to publish it.

And I will always be grateful that Angela Ajayi was the editor of this book. She has kept me informed and involved at all times, sending me alternative covers for comments, galleys for corrections, time-tables for my consideration, and suggestions for improving the text. It was clear that she valued "Oba's Story" and was doing everything possible to insure that it would be well-published.

Contents

Introduction

In 1999, Michele Gibbs and I flew from our home in Oaxaca, Mexico to St. Vincent in the eastern Caribbean. Once there, it was all but inevitable that we meet Oba because he worked from a vendor's stand on the busiest street in Kingstown, the nation's capital. Soon after our arrival, Oba saw us making our way through the crowd, fixed on Michele's locks, called out "Rasta!" and welcomed us to the island.

A few nights later, Oba and his wife Dafina invited us to their seaside home for dinner. During a long, leisurely evening, mutual friends and interests were discovered. We had lived in Grenada from 1980–1983 and Michele had worked as a journalist with Don Rojas, editor of the Free West Indian, the newspaper of Grenada's People's Revolutionary Government and a friend of Oba's. Dafina had grown up in New York City and Oba had lived there during the years Michele and I worked together in Detroit. Acquaintances, experiences and shared commitments multiplied.

The following spring, Oba invited me to travel with him though the Grenadines, the chain of small islands stretching south from St. Vincent toward Grenada. He had worked on most of them and seemed to know everyone. On Canouan, we visited with men and women working on a new luxurious resort. On Union, Oba led me through dry bush to a barely visible, decrepit house where he had lived with a Dread responsible for a quickly aborted military action against the government. On the island's coast, construction workers welcomed us with steaming bowls of fish broth and dolphin eggs and told Oba he was wasting his time trying to change Babylon. And on Mayreau, a dot in the sea with neither roads nor police, I sat with Oba late at night on a dark hillside, listening as he explained his convictions about Haile Selassie, the war on drugs and Vincentian politics to a gathering of skeptical young men.

He was born and named Richard Jacobs in 1948, a brown, West Indian subject of the British empire, the son of a middle class, civil servant in the colonial administration. He became Ras Oba Chatoyer, a black man, an African-in-exile, a Rastafarian and a political radical. Over the last thirty years he has participated fully in the religious and political life of the Rastafarian community in the eastern Caribbean, become an elder in their community and a public, controversial figure for his defense of the rights of prisoners, his work as a public educator and organizer, his protests against police brutality, and his commitment to political activity.

The dramatic changes and steady commitments in Oba's life and work occurred in the context of and throw light on the broader history of the social movements, conflicts and possibilities of our times. I suggested that his story was important and would interest others. Oba had recently turned 50 and welcomed the opportunity to reflect on the life he'd led and the future he might anticipate. This then is "Oba's Story" as I've come to know it, supplemented by my own reading and observations.

George Colman

1

The President, the Prime Minister and the Rasta

On October 27, 1979, the British flag which had flown for 200 years over the colony of St. Vincent in the eastern Caribbean was ceremoniously lowered, folded and put away forever. In its place, the colors of an independent island nation were raised over 100,000 descendents of Africans, Caribs, East Indians, and Europeans.

The British Empire had been withering since World War II as a powerful wave of anti-colonial movements swept across the world. By 1960, the English colonies India, Burma, Ceylon, Ghana, Malaya, Cyprus and Nigeria had become independent. As Eric Hobsbawm put it, "Unlike the French and the Dutch, Britain had learned by long experience in India that once a serious nationalist movement existed the only way to hold on to the advantages of empire was to let go of formal power."[1] The larger, more prosperous islands in the British Caribbean, Jamaica and Trinidad, joined the list of independent nations in 1962. Grenada followed in 1974 and St. Lucia, St.Vincent's neighbor to the north, in 1979.

Twenty years later, the Prime Minister of St. Vincent and the Grenadines, Sir James Mitchell, extended an invitation to a Commonwealth colleague, His Excellency Yahya A.J.J. Jammeh, the President of Gambia, to join him and all Vincentians in 1999 at the island's Independence Day celebrations. An African President would be an uncommon, highly respected guest in St. Vincent and a great attraction to the official ceremonies.

Jammeh had come to power in West Africa after a military coup in 1994. Mitchell got to know him when asked by the British Commonwealth to share his experience governing a democracy with the young African leader.

Jammeh accepted the invitation with pleasure and the word spread quickly through St. Vincent's capital city Kingstown, the villages of its countryside, and the smaller Grenadine islands that an African President would soon be with them.

Oba, a rugged, fifty year old Rasta, was exhibiting his books in the center of Kingstown when he heard the news and fixed the date in mind. The night the African President arrived, Oba intended to be nowhere else but standing by the airport fence searching darkening skies for signs of light, signs of a jet sweeping in from Africa, the homeland, the beginning and the end of his journey. Though born in St. Vincent, Ras Oba defined himself neither as Vincentian nor West Indian but as an African-in-exile living among the scattered sons and daughters of the great continent where all human life began.

He was far from alone the night Jammeh's flight approached St. Vincent from the east. Hundreds of others stood by the small, seaside landing strip, hundreds who shared common descent from Africa, hundreds known to Oba because St. Vincent is a small place, he grew up there, knew every corner of the island, and if he didn't know everyone, he knew a member of their family, one of their neighbors or a friend. All around him, people were talking and calling out excitedly, pointing at every plane passing overhead, warning children to stay close, pushing through the crowd to get a better view, wondering aloud about this royalty coming in from Africa.

Convictions, arguments, and laughter swirled: "Jammeh not a King, he a President, President of Gambia." "No, you wrong, he's not coming in from Africa, he's coming from Barbados. Jet too big for this scruffy field." "First African President to make it here." "No, Kaunda was here. I don't know when but he was here." And while all this waiting was going on, a few passed close to Oba, close enough to smile and taunt, "Why you so quiet, Oba? Police finally shut you down?"

Oba had been arrested a few days before on charges of assaulting a police officer; calling one an "asshole" had been the precise offense. The charges were dismissed but the Judge, tired of seeing him in court, warned that the next time he was brought before him, he'd get an automatic six months in jail. The arrest surprised no one. People were only surprised that

Oba was still walking upright because he was always in town chanting down officers by name for crimes against the people and certain policemen had been heard to say they were saving a bullet just for him.

Arrests and threats were not taken lightly by Oba and his wife, Dafina. They had four children to raise and guide as Rastas: Tesfa, Myra, Itara, and Askalae. They had family responsibilities and the work of socially committed Rastas so Oba did not want to get arrested, did not want to be tied up month after month in court, and did not flare up at officers unless seriously provoked. Given respect, he gave respect. His problems were not with police in general but with the very few whose consistently brutal behavior violated the lives and laws of Vincentians and had to be contested if ever an approximation of justice was to be realized on the island.

Opposition to power attracts trouble but silence and caution make things worse. Oba took the judgment of Frederick Douglass to be true and final, "Find out just what any people will quietly submit to and you have found out the exact measure of injustice and wrong which will be imposed on them, and these will continue until they are resisted with either words or blows or with both."[2] Oba had never walked the quiet way and was not, by nature or conviction, prepared to be shut down.

President Jammeh arrived safely that October night and was driven quickly off after a wave at the hundreds greeting him from the airport fence. A round of visits with island leaders filled the few days between arrival and the main event itself at Arnos Vale playing field, the large, attractive space on the southern shore of the island usually occupied by cricket and soccer teams. To the south of the field, a turquoise sea reached toward the island of Bequia, a dark shadow on the horizon, and to the north, green hills and wooded mountains swept upward to cloud-capped La Soufriere, the volcano which last erupted twenty years before.

A large crowd was guaranteed for the celebration because the great majority of Vincentians are of African descent and Gambia represents the land of the ancestors before slavery, chains, and shipment to the Caribbean. It was all but impossible for anyone on St. Vincent not to know about the special guest and nearly as impossible not to be interested. Television, radio, and newspapers spread the word almost as rapidly as mouths.

Security on celebration day was designed to be sufficient but not intense. Mitchell and Jammeh were leaders of nations and would be protected but in St. Vincent there was no need for sharpshooters with high-powered rifles on rooftops or heavy armor in the streets. The all but free movement of cocaine through the area had brought an entirely different and frightening level of violence to the island but the people involved usually had other targets, reputations were known and shared, and the behavior of the great majority could be anticipated. The walls between national leaders and the people were much lower in the small islands than in large countries and greater informality and spontaneity was possible on all occasions, a fact important to the movements of Ras Oba on that festive day.

If seated in the large grandstand on Arnos Vale playing field at noon on October 27, 1999, your attention would be drawn first to the many people around you. If Vincentian, you would know a great many of them and soon be involved in greetings and gossip, sharing the latest catch of bad news, speculations and dire warnings about public enemies and politicians. On the field itself, you would see thè country's uniformed organizations finding their assigned parading places: dark policemen, elegant and stiff under tall, white helmuts, cadets looking sharp in red berets, young girl guides enjoying themselves in short, blue skirts and tennis shoes, Coast Guard and Honor Guard flanked by the controversial Special Services Unit in green and brown camouflage display.

You would also observe two occupied pavilions on the field, the larger one for Vincentian leaders and dignitaries from other islands who had come to honor the country and its special guest. The other, more prominent pavilion, close to the center of the field, was reserved for the Prime Minister of

St. Vincent, Sir James Mitchell, and the main attraction, His Excellency the President of Gambia, Jahya Jammeh.

A ceremonial space had been prepared and all parts carefully assigned. The thousands in the grandstand were audience, there to hear tales of progress and to applaud. The marching groups were spectacle, entertainment and security, their military precision and character a reminder of the force available to discipline the unruly when and if necessary. The dignitaries from home and abroad played supporting cast and sat on a platform of their own, lending reputational weight to the event. The stars of the show, its leading actors, were the Prime Minister of St. Vincent and the President of Gambia, set apart, if not high and lifted up, on a center stage all their own.

Ras Oba got up early that morning and had a sea bath while the sun scattered early gold across the waters. Later, dressed carefully in the greens and golds of Ethiopia, he smoked the holy herb, read from the Psalms and prayed. He would, of course, attend the celebration of his country's independence. It was all but impossible for him to miss it because if Oba's natural place is anywhere on land or sea, it's in the streets and public places where people gather. He would be present, he would move slowly through the crowd, he would greet and encourage many, confront and argue with a few, listen to the speeches, and if the African President passed his way, he would quietly welcome him in the name of the poor and oppressed of St. Vincent.

It is the way Oba liked to move: a general direction for the day in mind and all the rest left unknown and open to the Spirit's guidance. He resisted imposing his will on events because he needed the leadings of a Power greater and purer than his own to keep on his chosen path, the Power that strengthens, guides, and protects those who are open to Him, the Power Oba had come to know as Haile Selassie, King of Kings.

He fixed the flag of Ethiopia to a long, thin pole and caught one of the vans racing down the sea road to Arnos Vale. Inside the stadium, he mingled easily with folks arriving from all across the island, waved to people calling out to him, glanced at policemen parading on the field, and made a point of speaking to the prisoners seated in a special section of the grandstand, prisoners who remembered that Oba had been a prisoner too and that in their recent, riotous protests against the treatment they received, Oba had been outside the prison walls leading hundreds of citizens chanting, "No Justice, No Peace!" in support of their demands for change.

Well past the scheduled hour, thousands of Vincentians rose from their seats and marchers on the field stood suddenly motionless as a strong voice boomed from amplifiers that the national anthem would be played. Oba left off talking with a young Rasta and moved away from the grandstand along the field's grassy edge. Somewhere along there, he thought, the President of Gambia would pass when the ceremony ended and it was there he would have the opportunity to greet him. Not wanting trouble and aware that security guards were watching, he stopped frequently and moved slowly.

Announcements and introductions completed, Prime Minister Mitchell presented his account of the country's progress during his administration. Oba listened and disagreed. He thought the majority of people in the country had little or nothing to celebrate, were fed up with the Prime Minister and his government, and would vote them out as soon as they were given the opportunity. Crime, violence and general insecurity were on the rise; the poor suffered want and injustice; unemployment and a hopeless future faced the majority of youth; cocaine dealers were buying officials high and low; an ever-weakened agricultural base meant more imported, expensive food; a bogus "war on drugs" was being waged at the insistence of the United States and St.Vincent's land, citizenship, and votes in international forums were being sold for cash and in-kind contributions.

Oba's believed that since independence in 1979, the politicians of the island, most of whom he'd known since childhood, talked progress for the people at election time but once in power dropped the people and made progress for themselves and for their class. Why had that been the consistent pattern? Why was it that bright, apparently sincere black men pledged to serve the people ended up serving themselves and the interests of commercial powers? Because, Oba believed, privileged, island blacks had never come to terms with their black selves. On the contrary, they looked down on their color, down on their people and looked "up" to privileged white Europeans and Americans. They were of the class that sent its "small island" brown children off to elite, white schools in America, Canada and England so they could learn to act like whites, get accepted by whites, and return to rule in the interests of the white privileged of the world with whom they identified.

In earlier years, Oba recalled, certain young members of this brown elite had clenched their fists, put on African dashikis, shouted "black power" and "serve the people," drafted and publicized the radical programs they'd initiate when elected to office. Well, they got elected, they got the power, they had the votes in parliament to enact their plans and they did nothing they had promised. Why? Because they were, when all was said and done, members of a privileged class that looked down on poor black people, looked up to rich whites, controlled, at least for the moment, the nation's resources, and had no guiding values at all in the use of them except the enhancement of personal power and privilege.

And yet only members of exactly that opportunistic, privileged class were representing St. Vincent to the African President of Gambia. Where and when do the people, black people, working people, unemployed people, poor scratching-for-a-living people, when do they get to talk to the African? Oba did not presume to represent anyone but his clear reputation on the island as an outspoken Rastafarian, an African man, a Garvey man, a "prisoners' rights" man, an "enemy of police brutality" man, a "some kind of radical" man so materially poor he had no lights in his house meant at least that he did not belong to the charmed circle of "important people" who had surrounded the President of Gambia since his arrival. His gold and green clothing, his beard, his floor-length dreadlocks tucked-up in a green silk shamma, and the flag of Ethiopia would say immediately to the African President that a very different and important segment of the Vincentian population welcomed him and wished him well. The conviction grew that he should speak to the African that afternoon.

He started down the field's edge toward a photographer standing on the sidelines close to the Prime Minister and the President. He knew the man and there would no trouble from him but members of the Gambian security force had been alerted to Oba's movement and stood just ahead, watching him and talking on their cellulars. Wanting them to understand that he was a friend and no danger to them, their leader or anyone else, he approached slowly and greeted the first Gambian guard in Arabic, "As Salaam Alaikum," "Peace Be Unto You."

Vincentian security watched all this, signaled Gambian security that they would handle the situation, and Oba was allowed to move further down the field's edge until reaching the photographer where he stopped and waited beneath the flag of St. Vincent. By this time, thousands in the crowd, alert to any possible excitement, had shifted their attention to Oba and the police heading quickly for him. But Oba made no attempt to go beyond the flags and the police, after warning him to stay there, made no attempt to move him off.

Opportunity opened its doors once more when the speeches had been concluded and the Prime Minister and the President stepped down from their pavilion and stood together on the field preparing to pass in review before the grandstand. At exactly that moment, the photographer leaned close and whispered, "This is your chance, Oba."

And Oba took it. The flag of Ethiopia held high above his head, he set out to cross the field but security immediately grabbed his arm and pulled him back while the crowd, watching the scene expectantly, began to shout encouragement. An attendant close to the Prime Minister called his attention to the drama developing on the sidelines and all eyes in the stadium were suddenly on Ras Oba and Sir James Mitchell.

Mitchell looked across at Oba in his gold and greens, the policeman holding him, the cheering crowd, and considered which way this thing should be allowed to go. It is not known what went on in the Prime Minister's quick mind in those few seconds but it is certain that he'd known Oba for a long time, long before he changed his name and grew his locks, and he could safely assume that whatever Oba was up to that afternoon, it was not craziness or violence. Besides, Oba was an elder among the Rastas, thousands were on their feet watching this sudden interruption and a scene was the last thing wanted. The Prime Minister waved at security to let him through.

Many in the crowd went wild with pleasure at the sight while others frowned and muttered, "Why doesn't Oba put his ass down in the stands where it belongs?!" But agree or disagree with Oba's up-front politics and practices, most people at that moment loved the man for being out there bold and proud, breaking ranks, out of place, walking and talking where he didn't belong and wasn't supposed to be.

Head high, his locks wrapped in a dark green cloth, Oba marched with dignified and measured step across the field bearing the flag of Africa, the cheers and shouts of fellow countrymen ringing in his ears, lifting him up, carrying him on. At center field, he stopped, respectfully addressed and shook hands with Sir James Mitchell, the Prime Minister, who introduced him to the President of Gambia to whom Oba extended warmest greetings in the name of the poor and oppressed of St. Vincent who were living for a time but only for a time in Babylon.

Photographers gathered quickly and caught the unexpected, dramatic scene, caught three men starkly unequal in privilege and power standing suddenly on a par, and saved forever the sight of one bold Rasta breaking into the closed circle of Presidents, Prime Ministers, Sirs, Honorables and Excellencies of the world. For a moment, the outsider, a strange Ras, a Prince, had entered the closed, curtained ranks of the famous and esteemed and publicly asserted his royal right to be there as a follower of the King of Kings, Lord of Lords, Jah Rastafari Selassie I.

2

Richard Jacobs Becomes Ras Oba Chatoyer

In 1948, Barney and Elsie Jacobs, British West Indians, gave birth to their first male child, named him Richard and carried him to the Anglican Cathedral Church on the island of St. Vincent to be baptized by a white English priest in the name of the Father, the Son, and the Holy Ghost. Ras Oba was not yet. Ras Oba was unimaginable in the small British colony and family of his birth. Ras Oba would not be conceived for another 25 years. Rastafari, a new religion, began in Jamaica in the 1930's but did not reach St. Vincent in any important way until the early seventies.

Great Britain had emerged as the world's largest empire early in the 19th century with colonies in the West Indies, Canada, South Africa, India, Australia and New Zealand. Toward the end of that century, Britain joined other European powers in parceling Africa out among themselves and by 1914 Britain ruled over some 400,000,000 people worldwide. All that began to change, however, during the Depression and World War II when anti-colonialist movements swept the British Empire into years of weakness and decline.

Richard Jacobs was therefore born a subject of the British Empire but in its terminal stages, a period of contradictory dynamics and signs. On the one hand, the St. Vincent of Jacobs' youth remained a land of parades in honor of the Queen's birthday and prayers for her well being, Chaucer and Shakespeare in the family bookcase, the autocratic rule of white administrators and white planter cronies, sailing ships on warm seas, cricket games, mountain wanderings, duppies in the darkness, and terrible "warning" stories about a disobedient black man's legs tied to different horses and the horses driven off.

At the same time, other stories were being told, contrary narratives circulating with entirely different messages. Like the one about fifteen black Vincentian women followed by 200 black men with sledge hammers, cutlasses, and sharpened knives breaking windows in the House of Parliament, turning over cars and freeing prisoners in the island-wide uprising of 1935. In depression time, terrible can't-make-it-time, black people rioted and rebelled in all the islands, raised up new leaders, organized unions, and moved against the white power of the British.

The revolt of Caribbean workers in the 1930s was widespread: strikes in St. Kitts, St. Lucia, Trinidad, British Guiana, St. Lucia and St. Vincent. Every British governor called for warships, marines and airplanes to control the rebels.

Total casualties in the Caribbean colonies amounted to 29 dead and 115 wounded.

What did working men and women in the islands want? Their demands, put forward during a Labor Congress of the West Indies in 1938, included an elected legislature and universal suffrage, nationalization of the sugar industry, prohibition of plantations larger than fifty acres, cooperative marketing, state ownership of public utilities, old age pensions, national health insurance, a minimum wage, a 44-hour week, and free compulsory elementary education.

George Charles and Ebenezer T. Joshua were two of the historically important Vincentians shaped in those struggles. They had gone to Trinidad for jobs and ended up working with Tubal Uriah Butler, the leader of oil workers on that island in the thirties and forties. Butler was born in Grenada in 1895 but moved to Trinidad soon after the first World War to work in the oil fields where he became a leading organizer. In the late thirties, Butler was charged with inciting riots and sedition but when the police came to arrest him, the workers fought back, men were killed and Butler went to jail for two years after which he was released only to be arrested again and confined as a security risk when World War II broke out.

In the early 1950s, Charles and Joshua returned to St. Vincent intent on obtaining voting rights and power for black people. In 1957, their Peoples Political Party won five of eight seats in the government and Joshua soon came to power.

Closer now to the spine of Oba's story, Joshua selected Barney Jacobs, Richard's father, a respected civil servant, to work closely with him. To know Joshua's politics is therefore to know a great deal about the political tilt of the Jacobs family and the social dispositions and influences surrounding Richard Jacobs while growing up.

In their book "From Charles to Mitchell," Vincentian historians Cecil Ryan and Cecil Blazer Williams describe Joshua as the leader who will "long be remembered as the most fiery enemy of British colonialism and the planter class; as the man who stirred the poor and under-privileged people of St. Vincent and the Grenadines into action for their rights as workers and as citizens."[3] In the early fifties, Joshua had worked with George Charles to organize "all workers employed in any institution, trade union and industry in the colony." Within a year, the new union had forty branches, 8000 members, and a political arm called the Eighth Army of Liberation. Joshua led strikes, fought with legislators and police, was charged with sedition and communism, broke with Charles, and got elected political leader of St. Vincent.

And it was this same "fiery anti-colonialist," this "enemy of the planter class" whose personality, voice and opinions influenced the young Richard Jacobs, not only at frequent political rallies attended with his father but in his own home where, late into many nights, Joshua relaxed with friends, discussed the way forward, and planned next moves. As a boy, Richard Jacobs absorbed the convictions of his family's political leader: St. Vincent should and would be independent, black people should and would lead, working people should and would be organized, black children should and would have the educational advantages the colonizers had traditionally reserved for whites.

Young Richard Jacobs believed all those things, had no quarrel at all with them, but his interest as a child was captured far more by sports and the sea than by politics, however radical, or by education, however fine. So far, in fact, did his interests stray from the academic excellence his parents considered fundamental to any worthwhile future that he became an embarrassment to them. He was a "Jacobs" and a "Jacobs" was expected to do well in school today and in a respected profession tomorrow but their first-born son did well only in sports on land and sea. Superb in cricket and invariably captain of the team, he was neither comfortable nor much interested in the classroom, studied only enough to avoid a flogging, changed schools frequently, dodged assignments, roamed the beaches, and dreamed of a boat that would get him out of there.

His parents arranged weekly tutoring for him with an Aunt in a wasted effort to get him on academic track. They held up his successful cousins as models to be emulated and considered sending him to live with relatives in Grenada only to learn, upon inquiring, that their relatives, worried about Richard's influence on their own children, wouldn't have him. Finally and somewhat desperately, they packed him off to school in Barbados at the age of 15. By then, however, girls had been added to sports and the sea as young Jacobs' prevailing passions and his energies ran even less toward the abstract and academic. His parents, more concerned than ever, brought him home.

And all this might have had a great deal or nothing to do with his development in later years but his parents' worries were altogether fateful in one important way: they caused his mother to take a firm grip on her child and tell him, "You and I are moving to New York City."

Large numbers of Caribbean people had been on the move since emancipation in the third decade of the 19th century because opportunities for work, income, and education on the islands, especially the smaller ones like St. Vincent, were severely limited. James Ferguson points out that 40% of the entire adult male population of Barbados left that country between 1881 and 1914 to build the Panama Canal. Across the Caribbean, men left home to work on the plantations of Central

America, cut cane in the Dominican Republic and Cuba, labor in the oil fields of Trinidad, and rebuild the devastated cities of Britain after World War II. Some 250,000 Caribbean men and women crossed the Atlantic and moved to England between 1950 and 1962, the year the doors began to close on them and the United States became the new destination of choice.[4]

By the late sixties, thousands of West Indians were on their way to the States each year, the number of Vincentians living off the island grew to be far more than those living on it, and Brooklyn emerged as the largest Vincentian city in the world. Richard Jacobs and his mother were among those who moved north in 1965, as fateful an event in the life of the young West Indian as it was a tumultuous year in the United States.

1965 was the year Malcolm X was killed, the year Alabama troopers attacked 600 black demonstrators on a bloody Sunday outside Selma, the year Lyndon Johnson pushed the Voting Rights Act through Congress, the year Watts went up in smoke leaving 34 people dead and 1000 injured, the year United States planes began bombing North Vietnam and anti-war protests escalated in American cities and universities.

Young Jacobs had some knowledge of the States before arriving but hardly enough. He had listened to a few taped speeches by Malcolm X brought to St. Vincent by an Uncle and had read about the Birmingham bombings in Time magazine but was not at all prepared for Brooklyn. "I was terrified, man.

Brooklyn was a jungle to me. In school, they put me back a year to study American history when all I wanted to do was play soccer." School in New York interested him as little as it had in St. Vincent or Barbados and within a month or two he was reviewing the limited options for a young black man newly arrived from the islands with little in the way of academic or occupational qualifications.

In 1966, he enlisted in the United States Army and did so eagerly. The military meant opportunity, independence, and physical training. It gave him a job, food, clothes, money and settled all questions about what he was going to do with his life for the next few years. Best of all, he was for once entirely on his own, free and far from family expectations and getting the demanding physical training his young, strong body craved. Basic military training at camps in South Carolina, Georgia, and Virginia was followed by the discovery of his appointed place in the great Army scheme of things. He signed up for training as an engineer but "knew immediately I couldn't cope. Calculus was way over anything I could do." The Army moved him into the food service program and looked more closely at his record. They saw that no one scored higher marks on the physical fitness charts and that few if any could keep up with him in a game of soccer. The army decided that Jacobs' service was to be on the playing fields.

Experiences and lessons multiplied rapidly. In St. Vincent, where his color marked him as one of the great majority, a majority with power after getting the right to vote, Jacobs had moved free as any man. Traveling with the army in the southern United States, however, he read "Welcome to Klan Country" signs strung across the roads and walked into and quickly out of bars that refused to serve him.

Northern blacks drew their own lines around him, labeled him "coconut head," "monkey chaser," "small island boy," "Jamaican." Moving with a group of brothers one night, a few of them jumped a white man for no reason he could see or understand, beat him up and left him lying in the street. Jacobs couldn't walk away. Jacobs wasn't brought up to leave a beaten man down and bloody in the street and went back to help. "Worse thing I ever did," he remembers. "They treated me like some kind of traitor." Trouble, arguments and fights of his own followed and one of several court martials came after a northern black came at him with a knife and Jacobs stopped him with an ice pick. Judged by a military court, he was found guilty of "assault with cause."

Relations were far more comfortable with southern blacks and West Indians. These were the men who became friends and guides to the 18 year old "small island boy" trying to find his way, stand his ground, and figure out how to make it in the army world. In St. Vincent he had rarely touched alcohol.

In the army he discovered Thunderbird and the pleasures of passing out with friends. In the St. Vincent of the fifties and early sixties, marijuana was hardly on the scene. In the army, Jacobs experienced, for the first time, the superiority of grass to booze. Before coming to the States, he had rarely gambled but in the army, the charm of cards led him to lose, effortlessly and repeatedly, all his money.

But over time, enough time, things began to change. In St. Vincent he had been neither a student nor much of a reader but in the United States as a black, uniformed, pledged member of an army waging an increasingly protested war against people of color in Vietnam, serious questions confronted, disturbed and finally unsettled him. Black, admired leaders like Martin Luther King not only opposed the war but called the United States "the greatest purveyor of violence in the world today." CORE, the Congress on Racial Equality, and SNCC, the Student Non-violent Coordinating Committee, condemned the country's aggression in Vietnam. Muhammed Ali, a great hero to Jacobs, told the world, "I ain't got nothing against them Vietcong" and refused to go. Stokely Carmichael, a Caribbean man from Trinidad and leader of SNCC in 1966, put Vietnam and Mississippi together in Jacobs' mind: white power tearing up people of color at home and abroad.

So what was the United States doing in Vietnam? And what, Jacobs had to ask himself, was he doing as part of its military machine? Who was he anyway? Who was Richard Jacobs and what was he doing with his life? What did he want to do? What was his place in the world?

And one day there they were, commanding every television screen and every front page: Black Panthers! Huey Newton, Bobby Seale and thirty black men outrageous in berets and leather jackets marching on the California state legislature with shotguns and M-16s to protest a bill making it illegal to carry unconcealed weapons. Other photos followed: Panthers distributing food to poor people and taking care of children; Panthers fighting for their neighborhood; Panthers calling all brothers to "serve the people!"

Jacobs looked at the Panthers and looked at himself, his uniform, his gun, considered who he was fighting and heard the question, "Whose side are you on?" He concluded he had joined the wrong army, was serving the wrong cause, and suddenly couldn't wait to get out of the military and do something useful with his life. He became, for the first time, a serious student. He read books about Malcolm, Che, Ho Chi Minh, African history, Caribbean history, his history. He read and re-read the works of Garvey, Marcus Garvey, the Jamaican who built an international organization laying claim to the inspiring history and destiny of black people, his people, him. He began to think of himself as an African and not as a West

Indian. He began to define himself as a soldier in Garvey's army.

Martin Luther King was murdered on April 4, 1968. On Jacobs' base, he and other black soldiers practically had to fight uninterested white soldiers in order to watch the national aftermath of the assassination on television: violent protests in 130 cities, 20,000 arrested, forty-five dead. Jacobs was shaken. "What kind of country is this?" He wanted "out now" and he took off, headed for New York City intending never to return but army agents followed and tracked him down in Brooklyn. Their interest? He was needed for an important soccer game and they offered him a deal: "come back and play and we'll charge you with being AWOL. Don't come back and we'll get you for desertion. You know the penalty for desertion?" He went back, he played the game and was honorably discharged in 1969.

In Brooklyn, the Caribbean heart of New York, he stayed with his mother for a time, got a job with a manufacturer, and caught up with his brother Laurent who had moved to the States and was already wearing the black beret and denims of the Panthers while selling the organization's papers on the street. Jacobs checked out the soccer scene and started working out with a team that dominated New York play, the professional club "Tafari." Most of its players were Jamaican and many wore dreadlocks, the first locksmen he had seen.

Given the quality of their play, he was proud to be accepted by them. The Jamaicans became more than close friends. They not only took him home to eat with their families, they shared their thoughts on life, values, powers human and divine. They offered him a different way to think about God and a different way to think about himself.

They explained that "Ras Tafari Makonnen" was Haile Selassie's name before being crowned Emperor of Ethiopia in 1930. "Ras" meant a "Headman" or "Prince" in Ethiopia so those in Jamaica who believed, as his new friends did, that Haile Selassie was divine, were called followers of Ras Tafari or Rastafarians. They opened the Bible for him, changed it from a book into a living word, woke him up at night to reason together over verses, to think things through.

In those same years, Bob Marley's voice was on its way around the world. His music touched Jacobs with "the force of liberation," drawing him even closer to the Rastafarians. Then coincidence: a Nigerian soccer player, admiring the way Jacobs moved on the field, called him "Oba" and said that in his country the word referred to a Prince, someone outstanding, someone fine. Soon afterwards, an African-American woman, without knowledge of the Nigerian's designation, also called him "Oba" but in honor of the prophet Obadiah of the Old Testament who was a "servant of the Most High." Jacobs treasured their confidence and praise but did not yet adopt the name as one he could openly call his own.

Stimulated, eager now to learn, committed to expanding his intellectual competence and range, Jacobs attended as many political education events as possible. He valued especially the work of two Vincentians living in New York City whom he had known since school days: Don Rojas and Samori Marksman. Rojas was an editor at the Amsterdam News and Marksman a leading political analyst and broadcaster at Radio Station WBAI. Each provided news, interpretation, and support for African liberation movements, the Cuban and Sandinista revolutions, and the emerging New Jewel Movement in St.Vincent's neighbor to the south, Grenada. Jacobs read what they wrote, listened to what they said, and attended as many of the innumerable events they sponsored as possible. They ran, in effect, a mobile, public, unaccredited and free graduate program in radical thought and action and Jacobs learned from everything they offered.

That Samori Marksman was a major influence on him is clear from Oba's conviction that the activist was "the most outstanding African-Vincentian of the 20th century." Born Stanley Marksman in 1947, his path was similar in many ways to Oba's: he moved to the United States with his family at the age of 16, he served in the U.S.Army, he studied in New York City and he became a clear political leader and teacher in the very years that Richard Jacobs was in New York searching for new models of black manhood.

Oba's political convictions conformed almost entirely to the positions taken by Marksman and Rojas. The only important difference between them was that Oba, seeking a "more spiritual way," moved on to become a Rasta, but a Rasta who combined admiration for a revolutionary like Che with devotion to Haile Selassie as the Light of the World. He took courses at Kingsboro Community College and studied Marxism-Leninism at the same time he was learning from Rasta soccer players and reading the Bible. He affiliated with the Caribbean Pan-African Association, he grew locks, and he joined the All-African Peoples Revolutionary Party led by Stokely Carmichael. And as he went along, the writings of Marcus Garvey occupied a place of honor in his thoughts because of the light they shed on the history and possible future of black people.

Garvey prompted Jacobs to reflect on identity formations, his own formation, the formation of parents and grandparents, the formation of Vincentians, the identities at the heart of a people's way of life. His parents and grandparents considered themselves British West Indians. That's what their passports called them, that's what the British called them, and that's what they called themselves as respected and admired families among the black British West Indians of St. Vincent.

Identified by the colonizers and by themselves as British West Indians, their lives were inclined toward all things English: Shakespeare for literature, the Anglican Church for religion, Jesus as guide, capitalism in the market place, Parliament in the Court House, nominal monogamy in the family, cricket for sport, and white as the color of privilege, if not quality and goodness.

Garvey's role in challenging the "English" character of such black British West Indians is nicely recalled in the story of a black Jamaican who returned home from working in Cuba in the 1920's and was telling friends about his trip. "Garvey common over Cuba," he said. "Nothing but Garvey. Anytime you hear a bell there, is Salvation Army or a man talking about Africa. Even the Cubans. I remember one day a Cuban man asked a Jamaican man what him is, and the man say him is English. The Cuban man say, 'You English? You English?' And the Cuban man laugh that day! Till I shame! Him say, 'You is an African, not an English.'"[5]

It was Garvey who helped Jacobs look with new, African eyes at his family and his years growing up on St. Vincent. He thought about the "Iron Man," the large statue of a soldier still standing in the center of Kingstown, the capital of the country. The inscription beneath him reads, "To the glory of God and Memories of the Sons of St. Vincent who gave their lives for King and Country in the Great War, 1914–1918."

Upon reflection, it seemed to Jacobs that a British West Indian could read that inscription and feel one with the sentiments. But an African? An African should give his life for the King of England? And what exactly was "great" about the First World War from the point of view of Africa?

He thought about the brown-skinned, middle class Vincentians who had gone abroad to white universities, returning only to rule and to serve themselves, men who had turned their backs on Africa and aspired, above all, to be proper "Englishmen." And he observed that when such privileged men took public office, their hearts remained with the white world, their solidarity with a rich, white international elite. To get elected they would say many fine things to black people but once in office, they would serve their own interests and their interests were with the white heartland.

Oba's own black, respected family had never been members of the ruling elite. His father, Barney Jacobs, had been an able and faithful servant in the colonial administration but was not among those with prospects or known ambitions for a greater role in the country as it moved toward independence. He was a "civil servant" when Brits ruled the land and he continued in a service position when the black St.Vincentian, E.T. Joshua, became the island's First Minister.

But while his father may have prized his identity as a leading Civil Servant and a British West Indian, he was never allowed to forget that he was not "one of them." Certain island beaches could not be used by him or his children in colonial days and the upper social circles of St.Vincent were entirely beyond his reach. If admired, he was admired "in his place." Barney Jacobs did well in the colonial administration because he combined the requisite virtues: intelligence, diligence, and obedience, which is far from saying that Barney Jacobs did not chafe against his assigned social place or detest the leash about his neck in the years before black people got the right to vote.

On the contrary, the fact that E.T. Joshua, a clear rebel and organizer of the poor, chose Jacobs to work with him suggests a man who had considerable sympathy with those who raged against the colonizers but who, at the same time, kept himself in close check because he had a family to feed, a reputation to maintain, and, no less important, because when he got careless and forgot that all men are not equal, he was forcefully reminded of his true position in the world.

Fifty long years after the event, one of Oba's vivid and disturbing memories is of his father, Barney Jacobs, standing at night in the pouring rain on a vacant street in downtown Kingstown looking for a cab when he saw the Colonial Administrator's car approaching. As a civil servant in the colonial apparatus, he was well acquainted with the Administrator and waved his arm to flag the man down and ask for a ride. The approaching car slowed, the white Administrator stopped long enough to stare at the black man standing in the downpour, and drove on without a word, leaving respected, admired, middle-class, West Indian, English Barney Jacobs standing alone and drenched in a vacant street on a dark night. The next day, Jacobs was reassigned and demoted. Lesson given, point taken.

Oba believes his father must have been drinking that night or he would never have crossed such a well-known line. But whatever the reasons of the father, whose thoughts are now beyond knowing, the importance of the event to the son is clear. Half a century later, the humiliation of the black father remains powerfully present in the son's own story, living there among the fires burning against the brutalities and hypocrisies of the white and western and Christian world.

So while it is true that members of his family served the English and called themselves British West Indians, they also knew their place was at a lower table and they dealt with that reality in many ways, one of which was by preserving elements of an African and oppositional consciousness rarely visible on the social surface.

One of Oba's "English" aunts, for example, wrote down, used for her own devotions, and passed on to family and friends this prayer for Ethiopia which continues to be used by Richard Jacobs' children. "The blackman is the Alpha and Omega of the world. Africa for Africans at Home and Abroad.

Let us pray for the success of Ethiopia against all enemies. Almighty and ever loving God from whom all goodness comes, thou hast promised . . . that Princes and Princesses shall come out of Egypt and Ethiopia shall stretch out her hand unto Thee. We humbly ask Thee to inspire our Most Gracious Majesty King Selassie I and give him the same wisdom and understanding that thou didst give and endow to Solomon his Ancestor. . . . Give our King (and his family) strength to bring about the speedy redemption of all Africa, endow them with Thy love against enemies, enrich them with thy grace . . . and bring them to thy Eternal Glory through the original Jesus Christ our Blessed Saviour and Redeemer. Amen."

Though no member of the Jacobs family, as far as Oba knows, was active in the Garvey movement, very little of the above prayer and certainly not the phrases "Africa for Africans at Home and Abroad" or "Our Most Gracious Majesty King Selassie I" could be drawn from the Anglican Prayer Book. It is known that such affirmations of Ethiopia and of the African homeland coursed through St.Vincent and the other English "possessions" long before independence and the "Black Power" protests of the sixties and seventies. And there can be little doubt but that these non-orthodox, non-British convictions spread easily and quickly among many who might not be inclined to endorse them publicly.

In 1919, for example, the Vincentian R.E.M. Jack reported that 475 men and women of St. Vincent had joined the local branch of Marcus Garvey's "United Negro Improvement Association." In the same year, the Governor of the Windward Islands banned Garvey's "Negro World" newspaper because its continued circulation constituted a "grave danger" to British rule. W.F. Elkins writes that 375 black people from the Stubbs District immediately fired off a petition to the Governor advising him that any outrages against Jack would "not be tolerated by the true and new Negroes of St.Vincent." [6]

Little wonder that the Governor of the Windwards banned Garvey's "Negro World" as a threat to island peace and tranquility. A threat is exactly what Garvey's followers on the island of St.Vincent intended to be. Consider it: some 500 black people, labeled British West Indians by the colonizers, had organized themselves as a Garvey group in 1919 and not only defined themselves publicly as "the true and new Negroes of St.Vincent" but sent a message to the British Governor of the Windwards warning him that they would not "tolerate" any action against the Garvey organizer E.M. Jack! This from "British subjects" of the world's most powerful empire in 1919. The "Negro World" might be prevented from reaching the island but the Governor was unable to stop "African-Vincentians" from organizing a strong, militant Garvey current which lived on long after them to nourish the Rastafarians of a future generation.

As a child in St.Vincent, Richard Jacobs knew little or nothing about Garvey, the United Negro Improvement Association, E.M. Jack, or the Negro World. His ancestors, however, certainly knew that a rebellious, outspoken group of Garvey's advocates existed on the island. And they certainly had some reaction to those calling themselves the "true and new Negroes." The least that can be said about their reaction is that one of Oba's Aunts was sufficiently impressed, then or later, to preserve a prayer for her own family members which included familiar Garvey affirmations about Africa as well as her own prayer that God would strengthen "our King Haile Selassie" so that he might bring about the redemption of all Africa.

One additional note on the Aunt's prayer. She is quoting from Psalm 68:31 when she writes, "Princes and Princesses shall come out of Egypt and Ethiopia shall stretch out her hand unto thee." The King James version of the Bible, the version she almost certainly used, reads instead, "Princes shall come out of Egypt; Ethiopia shall soon stretch out her hands unto God." Her insistence on adding "Princesses" to Holy Writ is a useful reminder that the Scriptures of all religions are kept alive by the interpretations of the faithful who, finding something important missing in a verse or teaching, insist, silently or publicly, on making them "right."

It should be emphasized that the Rastafarian rejection of European or Babylonian rule and their devotion to the leadership and guidance of a Divine and black African King is not tied to the hope that black people will have a Europe or a United States of America of their own, as if those regions were decent models in themselves. On the contrary, Rastafarians reject the United States and Europe and what they stand for as unworthy of imitation. The Rasta vision is not to copy them but to serve a new human order altogether.

Garvey was at once scathing about the values of the white world and hopeful about the role Africans might play in world history, "As by the action of the world, as by the conduct of all the races and nations it is apparent that not one of them has the sense of justice, the sense of love, the sense of equity, the sense of charity, that would make men happy and God satisfied. It is apparent that it is left to the Negro to play such a part in human affairs--for when we look at the Anglo-Saxon we see him full of greed, avarice, no mercy, no love, no charity. . . . Therefore we must believe that the Psalmist had great hopes of this race of ours when he prophesied 'Princes shall come out of Egypt and Ethiopia shall stretch forth his hands unto God."[7]

Ten years after his departure from St. Vincent, Richard Jacobs had become a revolutionary, an African, and a Rastafarian, grown dreadlocks and taken a new name as sign and seal of his radical change in consciousness. Richard Jacobs had become Ras Oba

Chatoyer. "Oba" to signify his desire to be, not a ruler, but "a servant of the most High" and "Chatoyer" in honor of the black Carib leader Joseph Chatoyer who led his people in war against the British colonizers on St. Vincent late in the 18th century.

Joseph Chatoyer and the black Caribs have usually been described as descendants of unions between the indigenous Carib people of St. Vincent and the African slaves brought there by Europeans. Ebenezer Duncan in his "Brief History of St. Vincent," for example, explains that in 1675 a slave ship broke up off the coast of Bequia just south of St. Vincent, its survivors merged with indigenous Caribs and gave birth to "black Caribs." Implicit in this line of thought is the assumption that Africans never made it to the Caribbean before the Europeans brought them as slaves.

A contrary position is taken by Vincentian historian Edgar Adams who marshals the evidence for massive Mandinga expeditions from Africa to the Caribbean between 1307 and 1312 followed by other pre-Columbian voyages from the West African coast to the Antilles, Central America, and the northern part of South America.[8]

Free Africans, Adams argues, landed on St. Vincent centuries before the British, united with the indigenous population, and gave birth to the "black Caribs" who fought the British as men and women of entirely free African-Carib ancestry defending their homeland. By describing a long, pre-

European history of African travel, discovery and settlement in the Caribbean, Adams lays claim to an ancestry for himself, Oba and all black Vincentians that includes not only those who came in chains but also those who arrived as independent explorers and settlers in the "new world" long before the British knew it was there.

And as Ras Oba Chatoyer, a free African "servant of the Most High" and "warrior against black and white oppressors," the former Richard Jacobs decided it was time to return to the island of his birth and "ground" with his people.

3

A Hurtful Time

In 1977, the word passed swiftly among family members, assorted friends and anyone else who might care that Barney Jacobs' son Richard had returned to St. Vincent transformed or, as some would have it, deranged. The brown, West Indian, middle-class, somewhat troublesome schoolboy who left the island in 1965 had reappeared looking like a Rasta, talking like a revolutionary, and calling himself Ras Oba. It was suggested to friends who wanted to see him that they visit Bongo's farm on the leeward side of the island. A Rasta camp had been established there because the food was good and the marijuana plentiful.

Oba had returned to where as a child he had always loved to be: walking in the hills above an all-surrounding sea. Walking now, however, with Rasta brothers intent on a pure and healthy life as far from the lures of Babylon as they could get, intent on learning more from direct, divine inspiration than would ever be possible from books.

There had been no Rastas on the island of St. Vincent in the 1960s but in the 1970s the movement spread rapidly throughout the Caribbean. Mario Moorhead of St. Croix wrote, "It was a heady time in the Caribbean. Imperceptible as dawn, irrevocable as day, Natty Dread emerged. While world headlines kept an eye on Grenada and the other on Cuba, no one noticed Natty boldly invading the consciousness of the young. Spreading truths and rights, island to island, he caused a generation . . . to embrace the unheard-of blackness. . . . From ghettos, shanty towns and villages, Rastafari arose and was quickly branded pariah, a fearful criminal movement."[9]

Those were the years in which young Vincentians returning home from work and school in Trinidad were heard proclaiming allegiance to the black God, Jah Rastafari, Selassie I. Their affirmations fell on fertile soil among young, poor black men because their social position estranged them from main line politics and religion, because strong currents of Ethiopianism and Garveyism had circulated through St. Vincent for at least fifty years, and because Haile Selassie himself had recently attracted a tumultuous welcome in Trinidad and Jamaica.

In 1966, "Time Europe" covered Selassie's trip to the Caribbean and published an article describing His Imperial Majesty's memorable arrival, "The frail little visitor, in full military regalia and a Sam Browne belt, stepped majestically into the waiting Bentley in Trinidad-Tobago's capital of Port of Spain. Thousands of cheering Negroes lined the streets, and one man gallantly pulled off his shirt and laid it in the path of the visitor's car. Later 1100 schoolchildren put on a dance extravaganza. . . . Thus last week did Haile Selassie, Emperor of Ethiopia, Lion of Judah, King of Kings and Elect of God, begin a week's visit to the three tiny Negro countries of Trinidad-Tobago, Jamaica and Haiti."

The writer reported that in Jamaica, " . . . the airport was mobbed by 2000 members of a minority Negro cult called the Rastafarians who worship Selassie as God and want the Jamaican government to send them "home" to Ethiopia. Prime Minister Sir Alexander Bustamente, 82, has discouraged such repatriation, saying wryly, 'We must protect them. They would just get out there in the jungle and be trampled by elephants and eaten by the lions.' Undiscouraged, the Rastas showed up at the airport waving placards reading 'Hail to the Lord Annointed" and chanting 'Selassie is Christ' and 'Welcome to our God and King.'"

All parts of that article are instructive, including the supercilious attitude of Bustamente. The important point is that in 1966, a few years before Rastafarians were seen in St. Vincent, thousands of cheering "Negroes" lined the streets of Trinidad and Jamaica to welcome Selassie, King to the Ethiopians, God to the Rastafarians. And, as in the Biblical account of Jesus' entry into Jerusalem where people spread palm branches before their Messiah, one man in Trinidad expressed comparable convictions by taking off his shirt and laying it in the path of Selassie's car.

Many Caribbean men and women had prepared the way for the Rastafarian's rejection of white as the mark of goodness, purity and truth and the celebration of black history, black spirituality and a black God. One of the more important was Paul Bogle, a lay preacher in the parish of St. Thomas, Jamaica, who in 1865 led black men armed with bludgeons into the town of Morant Bay to free one of their own being held in jail. Plantation owners organized a police action and marched on Bogle's village to arrest him and his followers. A shell was blown and black men armed with guns, cutlasses, picks and bayonets captured the police. The next day Bogle's forces marched on Morant Bay shouting "Cleave to the Black, Colour for Colour." They set prisoners free, seized plantations, killed owners, and took control of St. Thomas parish. A British gunboat rushed troops to the area, burned villages, hung Bogle and over a thousand other blacks.[10]

A plaque honoring Bogle is now displayed on the Court House in Morant Bay. "Here in front of this courthouse on October 11, 1865 Paul Bogle of Stony Gut led his people in a protest of the injustices to the poor in the courts presided over by the planter-magistrates. It was the start of what became known as the Morant Bay Rebellion. Paul Bogle, George Williams Gordon and hundreds more were brutally slain.

Behind this building are buried the remains of many of these patriots whose sacrifices paved the way to the independence of Jamaica. We honor them."

Marcus Garvey grew up in that parish and became the most prominent of those who took up Bogle's cry to "Cleave to the Black, Colour for Colour." He called on black people to think of themselves as Africans, to pray as Africans, to read their Bible as Africans, and to take seriously the expectation of the Psalmist that "Princes shall come out of Egypt; Ethiopia shall soon stretch out her hands unto God."

As noted, even Oba's Aunt, a member of a Christian church and publicly unaffiliated with the Garvey movement, had prayed that God would "give our King strength to bring about the speedy redemption of all Africa." Counted officially among neither Rastafarians nor among Garveyites, she stands for a generation of Caribbean black people who were making African sense out of their world before Bob Marley, Peter Tosh or Oba were born and thereby helping to prepare the way for all of them.

Unimpressed by their strange hair, their chants, their holy herb, and their black God, Vincentians were generally hostile to Rastafarians and associated them with theft, violence, Black Power, and uncommon weirdness. In the early seventies, the first years of a Rasta presence on the island, a State of Emergency had been declared in nearby Trinidad because of riots, killings, fires, and looting incited, it was believed, by the Black Power movement. Many Vincentians, up to that point only curious about the "jumbie" writing on city walls and the strange Afro hair styles suddenly popular among the young, began to suspect they had real trouble on their hands.

Then a visitor to Dominica, three islands to the north, was murdered and men wearing dreadlocks were arrested for the crime. Dominica legislators responded by passing the "Prohibited and Unlawful Societies and Association Act" which outlawed anyone "wearing any uniform, badge or mode of dress or other distinguishing mark or feature or manner of wearing their hair" and stipulated that "no proceedings either criminal or civil shall be brought or maintained against any person, police included, who kills or injures any member of an association or society designated unlawful who shall be found any time of day or night inside a dwelling house."

This law was interpreted by most people as a license to kill Rastafarians who, understanding the clear threat, took to the hills. Twenty killings followed during confrontations with the police.[11]

Vincentians had been even more startled when headlines in their own papers announced the murder of the nation's Attorney General by a man wearing dreadlocks. Cecil Rawle had been eating dinner at home, heard a knock on the door, opened it and got shot down. The murderer ran but the

Attorney General recognized him, screamed for help, and identified the assassin before dying. A reward of $3000.00 was immediately offered for information leading to the capture of the accused Vincentian.

All stores and schools on the island were closed as the "biggest manhunt" in the history of St. Vincent took place. Monkey Hill became a battleground. Within a month, the accused man surrendered, was judged guilty, and locked up. Although the man wore dreadlocks, he was not a Rasta. Nevertheless, the full power of the state came down on Dreads, Rastas, and Radicals alike. The government also published a list of 20 men to be prohibited from the island. Three well know Caribbean people were on it: Stokely Carmichael of Trinidad, Rosie Douglas of Dominica, and Walter Rodney of Guyana.

In the public mind, the differences between Dreads, Rastas, and Radicals had blurred. All three were filed in a conceptual bag marked "troublemakers" and important distinctions between them were ignored. They all looked different and dangerous to the general population. A letter to the Vincentian newspaper represented the views of many, "I have seen a lot of young intelligent men wearing a full face of beard and a bushy head. They look like a savage tribe of people in a civilized community."

Afros and Dashikis had become popular among Marxists and Black Power advocates. Dreadlocks, on the other hand, distinguished Rastas and Dreads from most political radicals and from the general population. But not all Dreads were Rastas. Dreads identified with Rastas' bold rejection of white, European culture and joined them as conscious and purposeful "outsiders" in what they also considered to be a thoroughly corrupt society but they did not usually share Rastas' religious convictions about Selassie.

Horace Campbell put it this way, "The obscene consumption and imitative nature of the petty bourgeoisie provoked a cultural and anti-capitalist response from the youths who called themselves 'Dreads' and who identified with the resistance of the Rastafari of Jamaica. These youths were rendered unproductive by the inability of the society to provide meaningful employment for them. Instead of chasing the American and Canadian embassies for visas to migrate from their communities, the Dreads linked their destiny to the future liberation of the region and to the liberation of Africa. Through the medium of reggae, the sounds of resistance were circulated and these youths identified with the force and energy of this movement, without the encumbrance of the deification of Haile Selassie."[12]

Disturbed by the pervasive hostility toward Rastas on the island, Oba did what he could to reduce tensions while moving with the brothers through St.Vincent's green countryside. "The whole idea," Oba remembers, "was to clean yourself up," an objective encouraged by constant "reasonings" together and by direct challenges to any and all behavior unworthy of the King.

So when Oba observed Rastas stealing the crops of small farmers and justifying their actions by claiming, "it's all Jah land," he felt morally bound as a Rasta to condemn their "pillaging." He argued that taking a little fruit from a large plantation was one thing but stripping the garden of a poor farmer was straight-up theft and good for nothing but insuring fierce and continuing antagonism. The Rasta way, he insisted, was one of right relations with all men, not easy opportunism and sloth masked as the will of the Most High.

Predictably, his criticisms were not received gladly. Offended, the accused launched their own attack. Who was Oba to be telling them how to behave? Who was he anyway? And, by the way, where does he get his money? And how did he get through the airport without cutting his locks when all other traveling Rastas had to "trim?" He had been born to privilege, his family had property, he had gone north and fought in the white man's army, he had taken up the white man's gun, he had probably killed Vietnamese! And yet here he comes, practically a stranger, trying to tell us what to do! The word passed rapidly that Oba was an agent of the CIA.

There were other disagreements. By and large, Vincentian Rastas kept their distance from "politricks" and had no interest in "armed struggle." The gun is the white man's weapon and liberation will never be achieved by imitating the white man. Liberation comes by separating oneself from Babylon and all the ways of the ungodly. The world will be changed when the Divine decides to change it and establish His Divine Theocracy. Until then, Rastas should go their own way, live in peace with all men, and not get caught up in futile politics.

It was soon clear to Oba that Vincentian Rastas were much less inclined to political action than he. Oba had been deeply influenced by the armed struggles in Africa against colonialism and by the steady stream of information and radical theory provided at educational forums led by Vincentians Samori Marksman and Don Rojas in New York City. Through them he had kept up with developments in Grenada where Maurice Bishop and the New Jewel Movement were exciting the hopes of anti-colonial forces in the region. And he admired the work of Ralph Gonsalves, a friend from school days who had emerged as a leader of Yulimo, a Marxist group organizing in St. Vincent. The vision of a socialist society advanced by the Marksmans, Bishops and Gonsalves of the world had become substantially Oba's own and his return to St. Vincent had been motivated in large measure by the desire to make some contribution to that struggle in his country.

To make that contribution, Oba had to know what was going on, had to identify the problems any serious political movement should address. He therefore traveled on his own through all parts of St. Vincent, lived with folks in "wattle and daub" houses where there was neither electricity nor running water, established "safe houses" for future use, worked with subsistence farmers, talked with unemployed youth through the long hours they had to spare, learned how the educational system favored those already privileged students who aspired to professional and academic careers.

He was eager to work on those issues with the men and women he assumed to be his natural allies, the Marxists and other political radicals. "Most of those in the Black Power movement on St. Vincent had joined Yulimo, a socialist organization. They had members studying in Cuba and between them and the New Jewel Movement in Grenada everything seemed leading up to the revolution. I was more inoculated at that time by Marx and the necessity of armed struggle and not really grounded with Rastas or the Nyahbinghi."

Contrary to all his expectations, however, Oba was not welcomed by those on the left. He had been away for 12 years, he had become a Rasta and praised Haile Selassie, he smoked marijuana and publicly advocated its legalization. Movement activists wondered about the stability of a man who had changed so much, judged his enthusiasm for Selassie to be counter-revolutionary, and considered his public use and promotion of marijuana a diversion and impediment to the serious, difficult task of organizing the people. Activists were polite but kept him at a distance. It was, he remembers, "a hurtful time."

By the end of 1978, his money was gone and Jill, his girlfriend, was pregnant. Her family sent a ticket for her return to New York City. Oba left with her. In New York, they lived with her family for a time, the child was born, tensions mounted, quarrels and fights broke out, and the police were called. Jill's parents condemned Oba for being quarrelsome and irresponsible—he wasn't working and wasn't contributing a dime to support his child. They didn't want him around, didn't want anything to do with him and asked the police to throw him out. Oba left, moved out, moved on.

+

Looking back on those early years in St. Vincent, Oba recalls a far more negative attitude toward women than exists among Rastas in the new century. "Menstruacious women" was the memorable phrase. Too many Rastas, he says, were "chauvinistic to the core" and he's grateful those attitudes have changed. The conviction then was that women, filthy with their monthly issue, drained men's strength and were to be avoided or kept securely in their subservient place.

The Biblical text cited to establish the link between menstruation and uncleanness is Leviticus Chapter 15, verse

19, "And if a woman have an issue, and her issue in her flesh be blood, she shall be put apart seven days: and whosoever toucheth her shall be unclean until the even, and everything that she lieth upon in her separation shall be unclean, every thing also that she sitteth upon shall be unclean. And whosoever toucheth her bed shall wash his clothes and bathe himself in water and be unclean until the even."

Nyahbinghi Rastas are, they believe, descendents of the ancient Israelites who were black people and they therefore read the Old Testament as their own history. They are people of the Book and read its passages as the word of God to them. If the Book of Leviticus says women are unclean during menstruation, then women are unclean during menstruation. Period.

There are, obviously, very different ways to read the Bible. To take one example, Ana Castillo, in her book *Massacre of the Dreamers*, offers an entirely different interpretation of the "unclean" attributions of Leviticus. She reads the book as the work of men trying to control women's greater creative power. "The taboo against woman's blood" she writes, "is inherently Judeo-Christian. In pre-patriarchal times, menses was the birth connection, a sacred element associated with agricultural fertility rituals. It is symbolic of woman's creatrix ability, once revered as magical. In Native American cultures, menses is still understood as an indication of woman's inherent power. But in the Bible, the patriarchs . . . taking material and spiritual control of woman's autonomy, her rights to the land, her children, made woman's blood forbidden, shameful and contemptible."[13]

Maureen Rowe, a Jamaican Rasta and scholar, has also observed changes in Rastas' attitudes toward women but notes that changes have, at times, been for the worst. Her research on the growth of Rastas in Jamaica indicates that in the 1930s and 1940s, women were not denigrated or assigned a subservient position but participated fully in Rasta work and rituals. It was in the 1950s, she argues, that the organization "Youth Black Faith" led a purge of so called "alien" elements and accelerated the male domination that became characteristic of the religion. To the Rude Boys of the 1960s, woman was "ting" or "beef" and the belief spread among Rastas that women were a seductive evil and source of weakness in the male. The use of the word "daughter" became generalized and the role of women shifted from "equality" to "helpmate" of the male.[14]

Oba did not and does not now share the conviction of some Rastas that women should be subordinate to men. He does, however, regret and condemn his own behavior as a younger man, "I blame the black man for the degradation among us. I say the black man is failing. Myself included. The black man has forfeited a lot of his roles. I was in that situation. I was a black man who had children but didn't support them. I can't blame nobody for that. I can't expect no other man or no other woman to look after a creation that I'm responsible for. So I always give thanks for being able to overcome that situation. My joy is being able to minister to my family through the divine inspiration of the Almighty. I don't know how I could be a man and have another man looking after my family."

"I know I'm behaving better in relations with women as a Rasta than I did as a baldhead and I don't want to ever go back to that behavior. Man, that behavior was a real burden and I don't want those burdens. In my pagan times, 'ting was to have girl friends, as many as possible, and kids whether you could support'em or not. I can't support that behavior anymore. Our heart and hands have to be pure, we have to build stable, black families and we've got to be open to new light. It's a sign of accomplishment just to be settled with the same woman. It's a sign of maturity."

+

In the early 1980s, Oba traveled back and forth between St. Vincent and the United States and was present on the island when, for the first time, teaching elders from Jamaica arrived. Just as the early Christian Church was shaped by the teachings of the Apostle Paul and the first disciples, so the Rastafarian Nyahbinghi congregations now worshipping throughout and beyond the Caribbean have been shaped by the teachings of Jamaican Rastas who traveled to correct, challenge, and guide those younger in the faith.

Because all Rastas are affirmed as priests living in direct "I and I" communion with the Almighty, there's a strong tendency for each to go his own way and create his own version of the religion. At the same time, there's a strong desire to "get it right" and establish some norms so the Rasta community might remain as true to the will of the Almighty as possible.

"Getting it right," of course, raises the question of authority. Who's to say? If Oba objects to the "pillaging" of a small farmer's crop while another Rasta asserts his right to do so in the name of Jah's revealed will, who decides? Inevitably, contending opinions emerged regarding diet, worship, the treatment of women, interpretation of the Bible, whites in the organization, repatriation, and involvement in political action but at the beginning of the 1980s, there were no recognized elder authorities on the island to settle disputes and set the course.

Aware of their need for instruction and guidance, Rastas raised the traveling funds necessary to bring one of the earliest and most important Rastafarians, Ras Boanerges of Jamaica, to St. Vincent. Miguel Lorne of Jamaica and Ikael Tafari, a Barbadian who had studied with Boanerges in Jamaica, were also among those who came to teach. Each of these men was and continues to be a major influence on Oba's life and thought.

Sister Farika Berhane has written about Bonanerges, the "ancient" recognized by Rastas as one of the founding fathers. In her article "Trod on Ras Boanerges" published in Rootz-i

Mail.htm on the web, Berhane writes that Boanerges was born George Watson in Jamaica, 1925. His mother, an ardent follower of Marcus Garvey, taught him early to think of himself as an African and to honor his maroon ancestors. His chosen name, Boanerges, comes from the Gospel of Mark 3:13–17, the passage in which Jesus "ordained twelve, that they should be with him and that he might send them forth to preach and to have power to heal sicknesses and to cast out devils . . . and James the son of Zebedee and John the brother of James, he surnamed them Boanerges which is the Sons of Thunder."

Boanerges first "sighted the light of Rastafari" as a teenager in the thirties and as a young man founded "Youth Black Faith." By 1947, his yard in Trench Town, Kingston had become "a hub for members and sympathizers of the Rastafari" and the place where Boanerges developed tenets considered fundamental to the Nyahbinghi Order. Demanding steadfastness to the cause of Marcus Garvey and a redeemed Africa, he called on followers to be militant in their fight against Babylon and to concentrate day and night on redemption and repatriation to the homeland. All compromises with Babylonian culture were condemned, including Reggae and dance hall music. A strict "italist," he ate mostly raw vegetables, fruits and juices.

Teaching African people to seek the light, to avoid party politics, and to find life in the fullness of Rastafari, he instructed Rastas to "Come out of other people's business" and focus on their own affairs. The return of the African to his spiritual heights would come when all energy was given to the praise and glory of the Almighty.

The high point of Boanerges life was meeting Emperor Haile Selassie at a banquet in Jamaica in 1966 to which selected Rasses had been invited. When asked by the Emperor why he wore locks, he cited Numbers 6:5, "All the days of the vow of his separation there shall no razor come upon his head until the days be fulfilled, in the which he separateth himself unto the Lord, he shall be holy, and shall let the locks of the hair of his head grow."

Working continuously to internationalize the Nyahbinghi, Boanerges met with students from across the Caribbean at the University of the West Indies and traveled to Africa in the nineties to strengthen congregations there.

Kerhane's description places Boanerges squarely in the "come out from among them and be separate" tendency of the Rastafarians. Oba remains strongly influenced by Boanerges and honors him as one of the Ancients. He follows his teachings on the centrality of Selassie, African spirituality, repatriation, and the necessity for a sharp break with Babylon but does not share his views on women or his proscriptions against political involvement.

Rastas and the Grenada Revolution

In March, 1979, Oba was in Florida picking oranges when he heard that the New Jewel Movement led by Maurice Bishop had taken power in Grenada. It was the best news he'd heard in years: a government committed to low cost housing, free health and dental care, free primary and secondary education, full participation of the people in the political process, and a mixed economy with a broader role for the state and cooperative sectors had taken power in the eastern Caribbean. His first reaction was intense frustration that he wasn't there; his second was the hope that St. Vincent would be next. He began buying guns for shipment to Grenada where many Rasta brothers had signed on for active duty in the People's Revolutionary Government.

Unlike leftists in St. Vincent who were inclined to scorn Rastas as devotees of a feudal despot, Maurice Bishop defended Rastas in the courts and welcomed them into the New Jewel Movement. By 1979, 400 Rastas were serving in the People's Revolutionary Army, a new development which prompted Horace Campbell to write in *Rasta and Resistance*, "Forty-nine years after the first Rastas appeared in the Caribbean, young Rasta brethren in Grenada showed that with ideology and organization, the Rasta can be mobilized to participate in a revolution. . . . That these Rastas were not wanting to go back to Africa, but were participating in the fall of 'Babylon' in the

Caribbean, was not lost to those who were horrified at the sight of Dreadlocks with guns. . . . Young brethren from St. Lucia, St. Vincent and Dominica flocked to see this new society where Dreadlocks did not have to shave their locks."[15]

By 1981, however, Oba was discouraged to hear that the Rastafarians in Grenada were being pushed aside by a faction in the Peoples' Revolutionary Government. Members of the Twelve Tribes in Grenada had called on Bishop to hold the elections he had promised and had been arrested for counter-revolutionary activity.

Campbell's analysis of dynamics between the Rastas and the People's Revolutionary Government follows these lines: "Local intermediaries of foreign capital . . . turned to fomenting divisions in the ranks of the Rastas . . . (and) moved to exploit the idealist tendencies of the Rasta movement, pressing two youths to denounce the Peoples' Revolutionary Government and Cuba.

"On Wednesday, October 10, 1979, (the newspaper) Torchlight . . . launched its most forthright condemnation of the Grenadian revolution, saying: 'Rastafarians in Grenada are likely soon to take to the streets in massive numbers to protest the debarment of Rasta children from schools and the arrests and charges for ganja smoking. This was told to Torchlight by two spokesmen for the Twelve Tribes of Israel, Ras Nna and Ras Ersto Ja Ja when they visited our office yesterday. . . . The Rasta . . . would like to know why the PRG is holding on to power for so long and what has become of the election promises. . . .

"These two Rastas" Campbell continues, "were being used as a front for elements who planned to assassinate the leadership of the PRG after engineering anti-government demonstrations. Full details of the plot were revealed after the regime arrested twelve persons, among them a black social science professor from an American University. The two young brethren were also arrested when the leadership revealed pamphlets associating them with planned attempts to overthrow the government."

Soon afterwards, other Rastas published a letter criticizing both the Torchlight newspaper and the two Rastas from the Twelve Tribes. "Brethren, Sisters. Us brethren in the region of La Digue ask in the name of Jah that in your paper I and I brethren would like you to publish this report for us please. Us see that Rastafari have made headline on the reactionary and backward Torchlight who early in the revolution call us brethren 'Zumbie in a PRG' and who had nothing to say during Gairyism Terrorism. . . . We strongly criticize Torchlight, Ras Nna, Ras Ersto, Ja Ja and any of I brethren who form reactionary group to assist Babylon downpresser man to take away us freedom. . . ." The letter was signed by Ras Kula, Ras Andran, Ras Lyon, Ras Umbre, Ras Pyta, and Ras Alan.[16]

Oba's view of the same situation is that after 400 Rastas had provided "sterling support" for the revolution, a faction within the PRG moved to denounce them as ultra-leftists, reactionaries, and CIA agents. As a result, the Rastas "suffered more under the Marxists than previously under Gairy." The so-called "People's Law" prohibiting the production, sale, or personal use of marijuana was clearly directed against the Rastafarians and provided the police an excuse for arresting almost any of them at will.

The larger problem, Oba believes, the problem that led to abuses affecting all Grenadians, was that the People's Revolutionary Government had a weak position on "basic truths and rights. The Grenada revolution was the people's struggle not Bishop's struggle, not Coard's struggle and not the party's struggle but a faction led by Coard thought they knew better than the people so they kept the people in the dark, killed Bishop and brought the revolution down. And that was the Beast's opportunity to rage, invade the island, and bring Special Services Units on stream."

The Grenada revolution was ended in 1983 by the murder of Maurice Bishop at the hands of his Grenadian "comrades" and by the subsequent invasion of that island by the United States. James Ferguson points out that while revolutionaries had taken power in Grenada, most other islands in the eastern Caribbean held fast to conservative governments. The St. Vincent Labour

Party, identifying with a middle-class law and order, pro-Western foreign policy, won over the left in 1979. Michael Manley lost to Seaga the following year in Jamaica, and Eugenia Charles in Dominica and John Compton in St. Lucia completed the conservative sweep. The invasion of Grenada by the United States accompanied by small military contingents from Jamaica, Barbados, Dominica, St. Lucia and St. Vincent in 1983 completed the reestablishment of US domination in the region.[17]

Dismayed by the destruction of the Grenada revolution and the hard hand brought down on Rastafarians by the Marxists of that country, Oba's sympathies and interests shifted even more toward Rastafari, Africa, and the guidance of the black God, Haile Selassie.

4

Groundings

> "To ground: l. To run ashore, to strand; 2. To establish (institution, principle,belief) on some fact or authority."
>
> –*Oxford Concise Dictionary*

Over the years, Oba has experienced both these groundings: the one like running ashore and feeling stranded, even lost; the other like finding truth and getting "sealed up in the faith." The first occurred in Vermont; the second in Jamaica.

Vermont

When Oba returned to St. Vincent in the early 1980s, he lived with Ruth, a Vincentian and Rasta who had two sons, Luca and Mosiah. She was also in the middle of a terrible struggle with Luca's father over custody of the boy. The court ruled in the father's favor and awarded the child to him. Oba believes the decision was based on the fact that Oba and Ruth were Rastas, poor, and therefore, in the eyes of the court, unfit to raise the child properly. Desperate, Ruth left the country with her child before the court had time to enforce its decree.

She had an open visa to the United States, got both Luca and Mosiah on it, mortgaged her home to pay for the plane tickets, and flew north with Oba.

In Brooklyn, they moved in with Oba's mother but quarrels with cousins already staying there prompted them to move into an apartment with other people. New quarrels and tensions, however, continued to disrupt and trouble them. Life in the big city was not working out. Vermont, where Oba had worked picking apples, seemed worth a try. They packed up, drove north, and stayed in a Vermont shelter until Oba got farmwork and Daisy Turner offered them a house near her own.

Daisy Turner is described by Oba as the woman whose strength and guidance changed his life and set him on a better path. Her great Uncle was Nat Turner who in 1831 led a rebellion of slaves in Virginia. Her father was Alexander Turner, a black slave who had fought in the Civil War then made his way north to marry Silver Bell, an Indian Princess. One of their children was born in a log cabin at Journey's End, Vermont in the year 1883 and named Daisy. She was in her nineties when she and Oba met and she became one of the great influences in his life. She taught him American history, stressed that many northern whites had opposed slavery, enlisted in the civil war and gone south to fight, so he had to stop thinking of all whites as alike. "Any little problem I had, I'd go to her and she'd tell me what to do. And if I did what she told me, everything went well. It was a crucial experience in my life. She helped me become a man."

Oba and Ruth were soon relatively secure with a house provided by Daisy, farm work for income, and their own garden for food to eat and sell. On weekends, they packed up their tomatoes, peppers, onions, and cabbages and drove to New York markets to sell food by day and boiled corn on the street outside major events at night. Sunday they returned home to Vermont and Oba's farm work every Monday morning. It was a hard, tiring seven-day work week but it didn't seem so to Oba because he was making a little money, he was farming, and he was supporting his family which soon included his own Vermont born child, Obadiah.

In 1986, Oba learned that a friend of Ruth's son Luca had arrived in New York City for a visit. The 12-year-old boys had been close friends in St. Vincent and were eager to see each other. Oba arranged for the young friend's trip to Grafton, Vermont. And on June 12, 1986, Luca, Ruth's first child, was accidentally shot and killed.

The boys had found a gun that Oba kept in the house, played with it, a shot went off, Luca died.

The people of Grafton immediately surrounded the shocked and confused parents with a community's care. All medical and funeral expenses were covered by donations.

Local clergy arranged the cremation and burial of the body. A memorial service was held in the house to which "everyone in town came" and school friends paid tribute to Luca. It was, Oba remembers, an immensely consoling experience.

Troubling questions, however, persisted. Rastas do not believe that death is the natural end of men and women. "We believe" Oba explained, "that a good life can conquer death so we seriously strive not to get involved in wrong doing." Death is the result of unrighteousness and any contact with a dead body is a defilement to be feared and avoided. Numbers 6:6–7 provides the text, "All the days that he separateth himself unto the Lord he shall come at no dead body. He shall not make himself unclean for his father or for his mother, for his brother or for his sister when they die: because the consecration of his God is upon his head."

But if death is the wages of sin, who sinned? And how? It was hard to believe the child had sinned in a way that warranted death but if he had not sinned, then who had? Ruth's question became, "Is there an unrighteous or evil spirit at work in the family?"

She wondered and worried about Oba's relationship to the boy, a stepson, and doubted that Oba had really accepted him, loved him as his own. She did not think Oba had killed the child but increasingly believed that Oba's thoughts had been negative about Luca in a way that weakened the boy and conspired with evil spiritual forces to harm him.

Like most farmers in the area, Oba had kept an unloaded gun and ammunition in the house. Why, Ruth demanded, had he brought a gun, a killing weapon, into a home where children played? If the gun Oba brought into the home had not been there, her child would still be alive. She remembered that Luca's young friend had been present in his mother's womb when his mother stabbed her husband to death. Could that event have had some terrible impact on the unborn child? Looking for answers, Ruth consulted a clairvoyant who assured her that Luca was well and would have died that day even if there had been no gun.

Luca's death, however, would not go away so easily. Something foul was at work in the family to cause the death of one so young, so loved. Ruth left Oba and returned to St. Vincent with the remaining children.

Devastated by the loss of his family and the death of Daisy Turner that followed soon afterwards, Oba "had to get out of there." But where to go for solace, comfort, community? He packed a light bag and flew to St. Vincent, imagining a warm reunion with Ruth and the children, starting over, beginning again. Ruth, however, had established her own new life. The Creator, she advised Oba, had sent her a comforter and he was living with her.

"It was hard for me to think through all that, hard to rethink my own self." He was almost forty but who was he? What had he done with his life? At his age, most relatives and friends had families, jobs, something going for them. He thought about his "nonchalant attitude about life," his lack of interest in "saving or putting up for the future." What had he accomplished with his years? Who respected him? His father had worked steadily and well, raised a family, enjoyed a solid community, "Dad was consistent with his work ethic but the only thing I've been consistent at was football and dabbling with farming. I just been roaming." Now Ruth turned him away. What was he going to do? What could he do? "I was in limbo. Some people thought I was headed for the crazy house."

His search for clarity and healing took him to Jamaica.

+

Jamaica

I and I scattered and shattered black nation,
shall never be restored
until I and I return with humble heart
unto I and I God and King

Oba went to Jamaica to visit leaders of the Ethiopian Orthodox Church into which he had been baptized in New York City. When he arrived, however, he heard that a Nyahbinghi was in process and decided to attend. In such a way, he believes, the Spirit led him to participate in one of the crucial events of his life. The gathering or grounding lasted seven days and nights and carried him from belief into immediate knowledge of the Most High, carried him beyond arguments, words and disputations into a Presence that changed and charged his life with the assurance of One who guides and protects those who seek to serve His Holy Will.

The word Nyahbinghi comes from the name of an African anti-colonial movement that called for "death to black and white oppressors." Death? "Practically," Oba explained, "it means death to the negativity whether it comes from blacks or whites." Oba is attracted to the African origins of the Nyahbinghi because while he honors the importance of the Rasta movement that developed in Jamaica during the 1930s, the word "Nyahbinghi" links the ultimate origins of Rastafari to Africa and not to dynamics in the Caribbean.

The gathering in Jamaica was open to the public and the presence of well-known Rastas like Mutabaruka and Miguel Lorne attracted many. Whites were admitted but not mixed-race couples. Women were expected to come in dresses with heads covered and shoes without heels but women in their menstrual period were not allowed. Men and women were assigned to separate quarters. Alcohol and meat were prohibited.

The gathering took place in a large, circular ceremonial center. Two wood fires burned continuously, symbols of the purification required of all. Three drums, the "true weapons of the Nyahbinghi," reminded those assembled that their fight is against wickedness in high and low places. The bass maintained the one steady heart beat; the fundeh's two beats called out "do good, do good"; and the akete or repeater, fired rapid shots at spiritual enemies.

For seven days and seven nights, Oba and hundreds of his new brothers and sisters smoked, sang, chanted, and prayed, moved in what he remembers as perfect unity, circled steadily together around the altar in the fire-struck darkness giving thanks and praises to the Most High for His goodness to His people, calling on Him to intervene on behalf of the poor and the oppressed, beseeching Him to destroy Babylon in all its wickedness with natural disasters, earthquake, fire, and flood.

Seven days and nights of this, seven days and nights of study and prophesying, drumming and chanting, interpreting the Bible and reasoning with men and women from across the Caribbean. "It's where I was totally sealed up, where I could accept the fullness and richness of the Nyahbinghi order and its power. I'm now absolutely clear there are no switches coming. Now it's only a matter of moving from strength to strength."

And the message is liberation, freedom from Babylon, freedom from captivity. Marley, as much as any one person, carried the Rasta message around the world,

We know where we're going.
We know where we're from.

We're leaving Babylon
We're going to our fathers' land.
Exodus! Movement of Jah people.

Here Marley has taken two pivotal events of the Old Testament, the Exodus from Egypt and the Babylonian captivity, and merged them into this one Rastafarian freedom narrative.

The Exodus, of course, was the movement of Jews out of bondage in Egypt under the leadership of Moses around 1250 BC.

The Babylonian captivity occurred much later, beginning in 587 BC with the fall of Jerusalem and the deportation of Jewish leaders and prophets to Babylon, an ancient city of Mesopotamia located on the Euphrates river about 55 miles to the south of present day Baghdad.

And it was there "by the rivers of Babylon, there we sat down, yea, we wept when we remembered Zion. We hanged our harps upon the willows in the midst thereof. For there they that carried us away captive required of us a song; and they that wasted us required of us mirth, saying, sing us one of the songs of Zion. How shall we sing the Lord's song in a strange land?" (Psalm 137, King James Version)

It is the same question Rastas face today for they too consider themselves "in captivity" and face the question "How is it possible to sing the Lord's song in a strange land?"

Oba's response is that there's freedom from Babylon if someone wants it, a freedom that begins not with rules and regulations but with the understanding that the Almighty and the Rasta are an "I and I." The individual "I" is part of the Divine "I" made manifest in the Christman's second coming in Haile Selassie. By experiencing themselves as part of the Divine Life that flows through all creation, Rastas immediately overcome the negativity imposed on them by Babylon and become agents of new, harmonious relationships with all people. Having realized their true nature, Rastas are able to move beyond the "you and me" relationships of antagonism and separation characteristic of Babylon and initiate new relationships of harmony and respect as the "Divine I" in each person recognizes, reaches out, and honors "the Divine I" in the other.

And though Babylon is powerful, it is not all powerful. Its darkness cannot put out the light. The prophet Isaiah's confidence remains true, "When the poor and needy seek water and there is none and their tongue faileth for thirst, I the Lord will hear them. I the God of Israel will not forsake them. I will open rivers in high places and fountains in the midst of the valleys" (Isaiah 41:17–18).

Oba is clear that until the final transformation takes place, and no one can know its time, the responsibility of Rastas is to purify themselves, prepare themselves, and separate themselves from Babylon and the greed, violence and inequality for which it stands. They will turn their backs on all of that and affirm their own black God and the new world order He will one day initiate. They will live as a maroon community "in but not of" Babylon. They will grow their own food. They will treat everyone as "I and I," speak the truth without deception, respect and protect the rights of all, clothe the naked, look out for the elderly, care for the youth and so live as witnesses to His Holy Ways until the last days come.

+

Dafina

Oba has lived with five women and is the father of eleven children, 6 of them born to Dafina. A son, Wesley, was born to Roslyn in the late sixties; a daughter, Yasmine, to Wilma in the early seventies; son Jarde was born to Jill in the late seventies; Obadiah and Wolde to Ruth in the eighties; and Tesfa, Myra, Itara, Askalae, Kaylah and Siyanda to Dafina.

Dafina was born Christina Marie Fisher in New York's Hell's Kitchen in 1973. Except for two years in Puerto Rico, her mother's birthplace, she was a New Yorker until she and Oba moved to Vermont. A gifted child, she was admitted to The Center School in Manhattan and later to the Arts and Design School on the basis of competitive exams. She joined the African Heritage Club, participated in street protests, danced to the music of Marley and Tosh and sought a "more righteous way of living."

She came up in a cosmopolitan, international world of art and music, books, discussions, and political protest. Black Muslims, Jamaican Rastafarians, Marxist-Leninists and all varieties of Christians were near at hand. In her search for "a better way," innumerable alternatives offered themselves, often too insistently. She refused, gently, quietly, firmly, to be rushed. She would take whatever time it took to find her way.

Her Aunt Jemalia, a Black Muslim and admirer of Farrakhan, with whom Dafina spent much time in her early teens was a strong influence with her clear African consciousness. A working woman, Aunt Jemalia sold goods in the Mart on 125th street across from the Apollo Theatre. There Dafina met a Jamaican Rasta woman and liked the way she moved, liked the way she encouraged Dafina to make her own decisions, liked it that Rastafarians didn't seem to be as strict as Muslims. "They didn't put any force on you" but stressed freedom and livity, natural living.

By her senior year in high school, Dafina had "locksed-up," spent more and more time with Jamaican Rastafarians, and felt herself growing steadily in that direction. A Rasta friend living in the Bronx introduced her to his mother, a Rastafarian who had come out of the Black Power movement. She helped the younger woman sort through the many paths open to a young and talented black woman in New York City. Growing ever closer to the Rasta way, she searched for an Ethiopian name to mark her new direction. Her friend suggested "Dafina," "hidden treasure."

Soon after becoming Dafina, friends invited her to visit a Rasta family in Brooklyn. She met Oba there in 1990. To say that she has been a stabilizing force in Oba's life ever since is to understate the case. Oba believes that in Dafina he has found his soul mate, the partner meant for him. They lived together in New York and Vermont for a time and moved to St. Vincent in 1991.

Oba smiling at one of his children.

Photo: Freddie Finch

Oba standing with Sir James Mitchell, Prime Minister of St. Vincent, and A. J. J. Jameh, the President of Gambia, in the anniversary celebration of independence 1999.

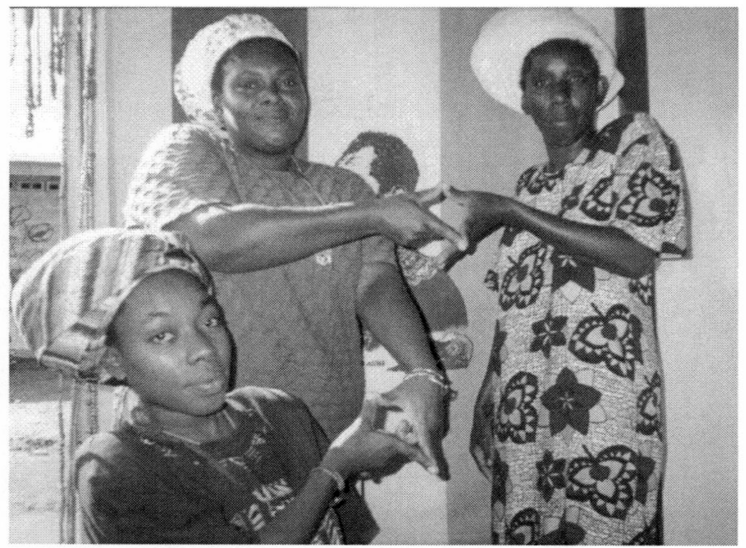

Three Nyahbinghi Sisters: bottom left, Sister Azziza Miyazya, upper left, Sister I Deka, upper right, Sister I Land.

Photo: Michele Gibbs

Oba looking out to sea.

Oba in front of a large banner of Marcus Garvey.

The new Nyahbinghi tabernacle in Oba's yard.

Dafina Jacobs and daughter Kaylah

5

The Black Lion

At the beginning of the 21st century, Ras Oba, Bongo Shine, and I-Man-I, each a manifestation of Rasta black consciousness in St. Vincent, worked together beneath the Ethiopian flag in the center of Kingstown. They occupied one of the small, wooden stalls lining Halifax Street opposite the Court House, the Prison, the new Market Building and the House of Parliament. Oba called that intersection of political, judicial and economic power the "Frontline of Liberation Square." That, at least, is what he tried to make of it.

Influenced by the world-wide struggle against colonialism, a movement that swept away the white colonial rulers of 40 countries and 800 million people between 1945 and 1960, Oba worked to continue that struggle among Vincentians by nurturing their consciousness of black thought and history. He sold T-shirts emblazoned with images of Che and Marley, books on Africa, Selassie, Malcolm X and Martin Luther King, and offered conversation on any topic. He also had compelling placards on display, so many that folks began to call his place "the cardboard factory." The featured sign might be a general one, as in "death to black and white oppressors" or dangerously detailed as in the one giving the full name and badge of a policeman who had beaten or killed a fellow countryman.

By the 1990s, he had become a committed Rastafarian of the Nyahbinghi order whose official creed, repeated with brothers and sisters on all devotional occasions, includes the prayer, "Let the hungry be fed, the naked clothed, the sick nourished, the aged protected, and the infants cared for." The loyalties of Rastas are with the poor and downtrodden of the world in whose ranks they count themselves. Their prayer is that justice might one day be done.

And the turn toward justice begins, they believe, when a new way of looking at oneself and the world is gained, a new consciousness that enhances a person's pride, dignity and strength.

Sister Azizza Miyazya, a member of the Nyahbinghi in St. Vincent, expressed it this way, "As we look around, we see a social degradation for black people and dis is why Rasta as a group come to bring to the people a way out, a way of life, a simple life promising the living in the highest sense. We realize that society has what they call classes and you find that black people are mainly at the lower level of the classes so Rastafari comes to show black people . . . that all people are equal in the sight of the Almighty so our teaching is for everyone, it comes as a teaching to show that black people can be someone. We recognize a black Creator and a black Christ. We are black and when we read the Scriptures we hear it saying he made us in his likeness and his image. If you're open-minded you will realize that they've used white religion to keep down another set of people. We are hoping to lift up a particular people to their better selves. So Rastafari comes as a groundation for people who are lost out there, like a rudder for your ship, so this is what Rasta do to alleviate poverty and social problems. We start from knowledge that black people are the essence of strength in the making of everything because in England or America black people have been the cornerstone of these cultures, black people have to recognize this and hold on to something black because we need our community, our culture, our nation. . . ."

+

Black History

To foster this empowering, black consciousness, Oba and other Rastas work together to organize Black History Month celebrations and lectures.

At one of these events, the public was greeted by a large banner stretched across the front wall announcing, "Organize and Centralize. The Rastafarian Working Committee presents Black History Month. 'A People Without Knowledge of their Past is like a Tree without Roots', M. Garvey. Organize, Agitate, Educate." And beneath those words there was a painting of the

African flag, a black lion in its center, and strong but manacled hands breaking free of chains.

The black lion stands near the center of Rasta consciousness, the black lion who breaks every chain and gives victory to those who move boldly. As lions, Rastas reject all "shuffling Quashie traits" and are able to do so because strength and boldness flow through them as a natural consequence of their "I and I" relationship with Jah Rastafari.

And the words, "Organize and Centralize" placed above the lion represent the conviction of Oba and many other Rastas that their strength will be multiplied when they get beyond moving boldly separately and begin moving boldly together.

Sheba, a Rasta woman in Jamaica, agrees with the affirmations of the Rasta man as Lion but insists on category expansion, "I am a person, not because I am a woman anyone going to think they can beat me down. More time, lioness more terrible than lion in the jungle. Without a woman a brethren is nowhere. Is woman do the planning and the fixing. She come up with ideas and him come up with strength and finance. Some brethren only want to reason up with them brethren and not with them Queen but dem soon find out dat dem don't reach nowhere."[18]

Sixty or seventy people gathered at this Black History event in the year 2000 to hear Dr. Ralph Gonsalves, a prominent politician, lawyer, intellectual and activist who had been in the political trenches of St. Vincent for thirty years. Gonsalves first caught the Caribbean public's eye in 1968 when he led student protests in Jamaica against a government which denied Walter Rodney, a leading Black Power advocate, entry to the island.

The audience that night was a cross-section of Vincentians: craftsmen, mothers, civil servants, lawyers, laborers, writers, Rastas and non-Rastas. Most members of the Working Committee were present though some opposed the selection of Gonsalves as speaker because his St.Vincentian ancestors came to the island as indentured servants from Portugal in the 19th century and not as slaves from Africa. Almost no one, however, questioned Gonsalves knowledge, his ability to speak or, if his clear ambitions were realized, his capacity to lead the country as its next Prime Minister.

After a period of Nyabingi drumming and prayers, a Rasta welcomed all and introduced Gonsalves, one of several to address the public that month. Gonsalves took the podium and talked to the group about three outstanding Caribbean leaders of liberation struggles in the 20th century: C.L.R. James, "the greatest intellectual the Caribbean has produced," Marcus Garvey, the organizer of the international United Negro Improvement Association, and Walter Rodney, the Marxist activist and historian whose "Groundings with My Brothers" remains an important text for Rastafarians.

The discussion period that followed was spirited. Some Rastas disagreed with Gonsalves' claim that Garvey had not advocated the physical movement of all black people "back to Africa," others wanted to argue about DuBois and Garvey. A local historian stood up and provided information about the history of Garveyism in St. Vincent, and a long-time activist assured everyone that the aim of struggle was and always would be "state power! state power!" A woman in the back of the room leaned over to one of the organizers and asked how long the discussion was going to last. The organizer assured her that it would go on until everyone was exhausted because Gonsalves was prepared to stay the night.

The next day, Oba was back on the street in front of the Court House, talking about Gonsalves' presentation, passing on the word, letting people know what CLR James, Garvey, and Rodney had to say about black people and their place in the world. This was his work: public education designed to increase black consciousness, a consciousness that stressed the proud achievements and traditions of Africa, the strength and dignity of black men and women, the power of black spirituality.

For Rastafarians, the exemplar of these virtues and strengths is His Imperial Majesty Haile Selassie, the Christman come not as a Lamb but as a Lion, a proud blackman mounted on a white horse attired in the regal vestments of a King and Ruler prepared to engage and defeat all enemies of the Kingdom. He is their Royalty, to HIM they pledge their devotion, and from him they receive their strength.

Visit of Prince Ermias

It was therefore an enormously significant day in 1997 when Vincentian Rastafarians were invited to meet with Prince Ermias, the grandson of Emperor Haile Selassie and representative of the royal line. Important because to be near him was to be near Selassie Himself but important also because his presence on the island would turn Vincentian eyes toward Africa and increase appreciation of their own royal roots. While non-Rastafarians might see the visit of a Prince as little more than the huff and puff of exhausted empires, those devoted to Selassie saw the visit as a way to expand a true, Rasta black consciousness among their people. As it happened, the visit of the Prince also exposed weaknesses and tensions in the consciousness and organization of Rastas themselves, weaknesses Oba knew they had to overcome.

The press release announcing the arrival of the Prince declared, "His Imperial Highness The Prince Ermias Sahle-Selassie Haile-Selassie is delighted to be visiting Saint Vincent and the Grenadines. The Prince, who is visiting friends in Canouan, had occasion to discuss with the Prime Minister issues of mutual interest, ranging from African current affairs and cultural ties to the Caribbean, to the situation of the Rastafarian community. His Imperial Highness will receive representatives of the Rastafarian community at the Prime Minister's office, Monday, April 7, at 10 AM. Prince Ermias is the grandson of His Imperial Majesty Emperor Haile Selassie I (and) left Ethiopia for the last time to return to school in England just prior to the coup d'etat which overthrew the monarchy in 1974. Prince Ermias is one of a few members of the Imperial Family who escaped imprisonment by the Dergue."

When Oba heard the Prince was coming, he knew it would be a once-in-a-lifetime event and quickly spread the word. The fact that Ermias had no power at all in present day Ethiopia neither added nor detracted from his magnetism. To be near him was to be near Haile Selassie who was and is God. Oba called Rastas on other islands urging them to come to St. Vincent the day before the meeting in order to ground with the Nyahbinghi brothers.

In the early years of Rastafarians on St. Vincent, there had been no separate "houses" or organizational differences between the Rastas. Over the years, however, divergent convictions led to the presence of four distinct tendencies: the Nyahbinghi, the Twelve Tribes, the Bobo Dread, and the largest group of all, the unaffiliated. Key convictions about Selassie were generally held in common but practices on other issues varied considerably. The Twelve Tribes, for example, have no prohibitions, as do the Nyahbinghi, against eating flesh, drinking alcohol or taking white wives.

Oba assured all Rastas that a new celebration was about to join the Rasta calendar that already included Ethiopian Christmas on January 7, the anniversary of Selassie's 1966 visit to Jamaica on April 18, Selassie's birthday on July 23, Selassie's coronation on November 7, and now the anniversary of Prince Ermias' visit every April.

On the night before the great day, Oba and the brethren gathered in a secluded section of Cane Grove to smoke and chant and reason through the night. The meeting had been called for 10 AM. At 8 AM, Oba arrived at the Financial Complex in the heart of Kingstown to set up tables displaying books about Selassie, Garvey, and the worldwide movement of the Rastafarians. On the nearby sea, boats were arriving with celebrants from other islands and on all roads leading to the city, thousands of Rastafarians and the simply curious were making their hopeful way to town where drumming, chanting, and the smell of smoke from the holy herb announced the beginning of a memorable day.

The center of Kingstown soon overflowed with Rastas in greens, golds, and reds, the colors of Ethiopia. Red for the blood shed by black people, gold for the wealth stolen from them, and green for the homeland Africa. New, strange, despised and suspect when they appeared on the island in the seventies, Rastas in the nineties were everywhere, generally accepted, and growing in numbers and influence because, as Oba puts it, Rastafarians represent the only alternative to doom for the youth of the nation. Though difficult to know exactly, he estimates 3000–4000 committed Rastas now living and working in St. Vincent, the majority of whom are not members of a mansion.

By 10 o'clock in the morning on that great day, it was clear that thousands of people had crowded into Kingstown's center to see the Prince, far more than any place could hold so questions went running through the crowd, "How we all going to get inside?," "Who they gonna let in to meet the Prince?" and "They should'a had this thing on the cricket field!" The word soon spread that only 25 people were going to meet the Prince. 25!! The crowd surged forward, pressed itself close to the building and the doors guarded by police. They'd come all this way, waited all this time, wanted so much to see! The police held the line, talked quietly, avoided confrontations, bothered no one with a spliff, and didn't want a ruckus but, please, some order had to be maintained or they'd have to call the whole thing off.

Prime Minister Mitchell's representatives circulated briskly through the crowd in suits and cellulars talking to known leaders among the Rastas and urging their cooperation: no smoking marijuana once inside the building, OK? Agreed. It was not the morning for a confrontation. But still, who gets inside? And who makes that decision? Oba and his brethren had been up all night preparing for the meeting but they had not prepared an answer to that obviously important question. It was to be, finally, the Prime Minister's call. He had invited the Prince to St. Vincent, he had arranged the meeting, and he usually knew what he wanted and how to get it.

The Prime Minister selected Ras Shaka to choose the 25 Rastas to be allowed inside to meet the Prince. He also instructed Shaka to read the list out in front of the assembled crowd so police and everybody else would know who was and who wasn't going through that door.

Oba, whose name was among the 25, was embarrassed by the whole procedure and the denied expectations of so many people. He knew that a Council of Elders should have thought things through and made decisions long before such confusion and bad feelings got generated but the sad truth was that no Council of Elders existed among the Nyabinghi because a major dispute had taken place that had to get resolved if Rastas were going to make their own decisions and not have to stand awkwardly by while the Prime Minister moved them around like pawns.

It is worth noting that however much speculation and contention there had been among the gathered Rastas about who would be on the list of 25 to see the Prince, it had been assumed by almost all that Oba would be among the chosen, almost had to be among them because he had grown far beyond the young, unsettled Rasta of the seventies and become widely known as one of the most outspoken, controversial, and generally respected elders among the Rastafarians of St. Vincent.

The actual meeting with Prince Ermias proved to be more a cordial ceremonial occasion than an opportunity for genuine interchange. The 25 selected Rastas all knew each other but they were in no sense a delegation representing Rastafari on the island. They had not met to discuss the meeting, prepare an agenda or determine concerns they wanted to discuss and were therefore unable to advocate positions or guide proceedings. The presence of the Prime Minister, various members of his government and a number of reporters further inhibited the expression of opinions and questions which might have been put forward had they been alone with the Prince.

Given the lack of preparation, there had inevitably been awkward moments. When the Prime Minister entered the room, he glanced immediately about at the seated Rastas and challenged, "You're not standing when the Prime Minister of your country enters the room?" Not wanting anything to mar the visit of the Prince, the Rastas slowly rose.

In the meeting itself, the Prince announced it was his pleasure to assure the Rastas that from that day forward the hair of Rastas would not be trimmed or cut off while in jail.

This had been a demand of the Rastas for many years because their locks were immediately cut off upon detention, usually on charges related to marijuana, and their hair was far more than a style. Their dreadlocks were an affirmation of faith, the mark of their separation from Babylon, a sign of their adherence to Biblical prohibitions. For some Rastas, their locks were antenna linking them to movements and messages of divine forces. To cut them off was not a haircut, it was a violation of their religion. The announcement of the Prince would be important to every Rasta on the island.

But Prime Minister Mitchell interrupted before the Prince finished and explained that Rastas' hair would no longer be trimmed on "remand" or when a Rasta's case had not been settled and he was not in jail, but would continue to be cut when imprisoned. It is certain that if such "news" had been announced by the Prime Minister at any other time or in any other meeting, Oba and others would have been on their feet objecting vigorously because the conditions promised were exactly the conditions already established. The locks of Rastas would continue to be cut if in jail but not while out of it waiting for a court date. There was nothing new at all in the announcement but, once again, it was not the time or place to say anything possibly embarrassing to the Prince so the Rastas kept quiet.

All awkward moments aside, it remained a memorable morning: thousands of Rastas had filled the center of Kingstown and 25 of them had learned more about conditions in Ethiopia. They were pleased the Prince had expressed his desire to return for a longer visit, and they were grateful to have been in the presence of Ethiopian royalty. Oba gave thanks for being there because "we knew that Selassie I himself was an invisible presence in the room."

The excluded brothers outside on the street, however, were not at all pleased and were outspoken in their anger. They accused certain Rastas of being "egos on parade" and threatened to have no more to do with them. Oba spoke directly after the meeting to Ras Bones, the priest of the Nyahbinghi at that time, and asked for a meeting at which the whole affair could be discussed: arrangements, agenda, selection of participants, and the creation of a Council of Elders able to speak and plan in the name of the Rastafari so that such a meeting never happened that way again.

It was soon recognized by Rastas that they had gained almost nothing from the meeting: there had been no real interaction with the Prince, no changes in the diet of imprisoned Rastas, no change in the practice of cutting off locks when jailed, and no change in the criminalization of marijuana. Mitchell had used Ras Shaka for his own purposes, extended invitations through him, selected the 25 through him, and controlled the agenda from beginning to end. No important issues had been raised, the Rastas outside had been alienated by the procedure, the drums had not arrived on time, even the Nyahbinghi priest came late and was judged disrespectful to the Royal.

Immediately afterwards, serious conflict broke out among the Nyahbinghi over the use of land granted them in Cane Grove by the government. Because no Nyahbinghi Council of Elders existed at the time of the grant, the High Priest of the Nyahbinghi had taken the initiative and signed all legal documents himself thereby becoming the official recipient of the property.

When disputes subsequently arose between Rastas about how to use the land, the Priest claimed both the legal and moral right to decide. In the ensuing conflict, the Priest was accused of immorality, the tabernacle was set on fire, the police were called and the problem ended up in court. As a result, relations between contending Rastas were fractured, no Council of Elders existed capable of healing the wounds, and the Tabernacle itself had become a center of strife and therefore unusable as a place for the worship of the Almighty. Oba was among the brothers who read these "signs of the times" and committed themselves to the creation of a new tabernacle in a new place so that a new unity among Rastas would made it possible to "move boldly together."

6

Prisoners, Death and Drugs

Since their beginnings in the 1930s, Rastas have been especially sensitive and articulate about the public and private abuse of citizens because they, as Rastas, have so often been on the receiving end of bitterness and hostility.

They have been particularly concerned about conditions in prisons because they have so often been confined there on charges of possessing marijuana.

And they have been denied the open use of their sacrament, the holy herb, in the name of a bogus War on Drugs.

The Prisoners' Rebellion

Oba's concern for prisoners goes beyond the treatment of Rastas. He believes that people should pay for crimes committed but that the right to humane treatment should not stop at prison doors. Prisoners are commonly judged by the public to deserve whatever treatment they get in jail and prisoners' "protests" are scorned by a large swath of Vincentian society.

Oba is committed to the principle that all human rights should be respected in all places and all the time and should be especially guarded when anyone is defenseless against attacks and outrages. It was therefore natural, even necessary for him to respond in the fall of 1999 when prisoners rioted in what Vincentians still call "her Majesty's prison." Their protest was stirred by the rotten, putrid food they had to eat, by the absence of medical attention when they were sick or injured, and by the overcrowded cells in which youthful, one-time offenders were mixed with the dangerous and violent.

The absence of any response to prisoners' repeated complaints led, finally, to an eruption. Prisoners set the place on fire, threw whatever they could lay their hands on into the courtyard, scaled prison walls and took positions on the roof where they shouted to the gathering public. An emergency was declared and the Special Services Unit called in to stifle the protest and shut the problem down.

Working in the center of town directly across the street from the prison, Oba was aware of the rebellion as soon as it exploded. His immediate response was to move through the streets of Kingstown organizing hundreds of citizens to march around the prison chanting, "No Justice, No Peace!!" to express support for the correction of prisoners' grievances.

Everything Oba had learned in New York City during protests against the war in Vietnam or marching with Black Men Against Crack was put to use. The placards carried were readable from a distance, confrontations with the police were avoided, discipline was maintained, and provocateurs were weeded out. Valuable in itself, the demonstration supporting prisoners' complaints was for Oba also an organizing and training event in which Vincentians gained valuable political experience and education through their public support of "sufferers."

Oba is clearly a leader in such events but does not think of himself as a leader nor does he aspire to be one. He thinks of himself as a political educator and organizer and as a good #2 man if the right leader ever came along.

And because he considers himself an educator and organizer and not an aspiring leader or politician, Oba is not overly concerned about how the general public reacts to what he does. He knows that some consider him unnecessarily quarrelsome and accuse him of stirring up trouble where there isn't any. He's aware of the accusation that he supports "rioting by prisoners." And though he's always ready to discuss what he and others were doing outside the jail while those inside were burning it down, he's far more interested in the impact the demonstration had on the demonstrators themselves because those were the people in motion, those were the people actually doing something to advance human rights and therefore those especially important to the future of justice in St. Vincent.

Oba moves freely and spontaneously on the island in part because he is not a would-be leader or a candidate for public office counting votes. Free of those encumbrances, he uses various approaches to advance his central work of organizing and educating: public drama, street theatre, drawing others into action on a public stage so they might see the world from a different point of view and tell a different story to friends and neighbors about, for instance, prisoners and human rights.

It is in the spirit of a public educator that Oba takes books from his own library and carries them to "Liberation Square" so people can pick them up and read, puts the Ethiopian flag above his vendor's stall, smokes ganja directly and openly across from Parliament, and calls for the recognition of the rebel leader Chatoyer as St.Vincent's national hero. Some are offended by his public displays and consider him a troublesome loudmouth. Those more sympathetic to his causes might describe him as a town crier spreading the news or as a working journalist plying his trade with cardboard signs identifying by name and badge number policemen guilty of brutality and murder.

In 2003, a new police commissioner is on the scene and has offered to take Oba through the prisons in order to sort through existing problems. The Nyahbinghi plan to visit those Rastas now in jail, deliver needed supplies, sharing Rasta news and literature. Presentations on Black History might follow with speakers, films, books and conversations designed to help "those in prison overcome the negativity they carry about themselves."

The Death of David Browne

On March 9, 2000, Oba and Bongo Shine were busy hanging a huge painting of Marcus Garvey on the wrought-iron fence in front of the nation's Court House and Parliament building. The "Queen's Wall" was used regularly by Oba as a community bulletin board. The message provided the public that day was Garvey's exhortation to all black people, "Be as proud of your race today as our fathers were in the days of yore. We have a beautiful history and we shall create another in the future that will astonish the world."

Before the day ended, a different, terrible message would be posted on the same fence beside Garvey's image because within hours a woman was seen hurrying through crowded streets to tell Oba that Rasta David Browne, a member of the Twelve Tribes, had been murdered by police.

The newspaper Searchlight reported Browne's death with massive headlines, "KILLED IN CUSTODY," and described the event in important detail. "Controversy has once more erupted over the death of a civilian allegedly shot by the police. David Browne is said to have died from a gunshot wound to the head shortly after the police arrested him. Reports are that the 35 year old man of Long Wall succumbed to a bullet wound to the left side of his head shortly after he was allegedly beaten and thrown into a black police jeep by members of the Special Services Unit."

"An eyewitness, who prefers to remain anonymous, said Browne, who lived in a shack close to the river at the back of the Prep School was straightening some nails when three officers, the principal of the St. Vincent Grammar School and another individual approached him. 'They went to him and called him, he put down the piece of steel and went to them. They told him it's against the law to build there. He said he is a poor man and doesn't have anywhere to live. They then told him they were going to lock him up. . . .

"As Browne was placed in the police transport the eyewitness said he pointed out to the officers that he did not do anything. It is alleged that a struggle ensued between Browne and the officers and he kicked one of the officers in his face. The source stated that one of the officers responded by withdrawing his gun, cranked it and hit him several times over his body then I heard when the bullet went off. One of the officers just walked away and the man that was standing there held his head. . . ."

"Police Commissioner Osborne Quow...said an inquest would be held soon . . . However when Searchlight tried to reach him to find out how soon the inquest and investigation would start . . . his office referred us to the Deputy Police Commissioner who then referred us to the Police Public Relations Officer who had said earlier the matter is out of their hands."

In the year before Browne's death, public protests about police behavior in St. Vincent had so increased that the Police Commissioner established a Police Public Relations and Complaints Office "to amend the friction that has developed between the public and the Force over the years." Police "friction" with the public included a long list of protests from Vincentians outraged by police breaking into their homes, intimidating men, women and children, brutally beating suspects, and killing members of their family who had been in police custody.

On call-in radio, a mother condemned police for coming into her home, arresting her daughter and taking her to the station dressed only in "shirt and panties." A garage owner reported a policeman came into his garage with gun drawn and told him he was under arrest but gave no charges, put him in cuffs and carried him to the station where he had to wait for half-a-day before being released. Bongo Shaka reported that up and down the island the police were stopping Rastas, grabbing them by the locks and jerking them around.

Oba knew what they were talking about. He had enough bitter experiences with police intimidations, humiliations, raids and searches to keep him angry and alert all the time. Walking down Kingstown's main street in plain view of the Court House one day, a policeman rushed him, grabbed him by the seat of the pants, and started pushing him through the crowd, saying

Oba was under arrest because there was a bench warrant out for him. Oba told the officer not to jerk him around like that because he'd go freely with him to get the matter straightened out. On arrival at the station, Oba was searched, his money taken out of his pocket, his glasses taken away, and he was told to sit down and be quiet. An hour later a different officer explained that no bench warrant existed and he could go.

Oba wrote the Police, the local Human Rights Association, the Public Service Commission, and the U.N. Human Rights Department describing the false arrest and asking, "Do the police of any country have the right to disrespect the rights of citizens? Does the premise that a person is innocent until proven guilty have no validity in this nation so that an innocent bystander can be readily arrested without any common courtesy?"

A more ominous attack came at 3 AM one night. Oba woke up suddenly, heard strange noises outside, jumped out of bed, looked cautiously through the windows and saw 15 or 20 men with automatic weapons and bulletproof vests surrounding his home. Some were already trying to break through the front door with a crow bar. Afraid for his children, he shouted that he'd come out with his family. He and the frightened children then waited in the rain while uniformed, heavily armed policemen with no search warrant and no legal right to be there, went through closets, drawers, cupboards, and files looking for drugs, arms, or anything else they could use against him. They found nothing.

Why had they come with automatic weapons in the middle of the night and forced their way into his home? Almost certainly because Oba had gone to Police Headquarters a few days earlier and publicly called for the suspension of two policemen who had roughed him up. The police returned at 3 AM a few nights later to deliver their own message: "Oba, you're small and weak. We're strong. You make trouble, you get trouble. Keep out of the way or we'll take you out of the way."

Caspar London, a columnist for the Vincentian News, reviewed community protests against out-of-control police and wrote ". . . the country is heading towards a serious bloody confrontation between the police and a section of this country's citizens and the goodwill which existed in the past between the community and the police is being systematically destroyed by the recent killings of persons in police custody. . . . David Browne, the latest victim to die in police custody after being arrested without any resistance and put into the police transport, is supposed to have kicked an officer and then ended up with a bullet in his head. . . . I am making a passionate plea to readers of this column to see that justice is done in the case of David Browne. A stopping should be put to the wanton slaughter of civilians in police custody."

And where was Oba in all of this? What did the Rastas do when a member of the Twelve Tribes was killed? Word of David Browne's death reached Oba within hours of the event. He immediately searched for and found a woman who had witnessed the death scene and who identified an officer of the Special Services Unit as the man who had shot and killed Browne. She was not, understandably, prepared to speak publicly until she talked with an attorney. Oba then went with Ras Levi to a leading radio station and told Glen Jackson, the anchor of a popular program, what an eye-witness had seen and called for an immediate investigation of the murder. Jackson called the Police Public Relations Officer and was told that the principal of the school had been on the scene and described the death as "accidental."

Oba knew immediately that a public relations story designed "to minimize damage" at whatever cost to truth had been concocted and put in circulation so he went to the principal of the school who had witnessed the event. The school administrator said the police officer had not intended to kill Browne. The gun had gone off accidentally. Oba challenged the principal's ability to know what the officer intended. "You have no way of knowing what was in his mind. He shot him, the man's dead, of course he claims it was an accident."

Browne's mother arrived as soon as possible from Trinidad where she had lived since 1977 and was taken directly to Oba because family friends told her he was the man to see. Oba took her to Commissioner of Police Quow. Accompanied by relatives, Oba and Browne's mother climbed three flights of stairs to the Commissioner's office only to be told they had to go to the Public Relations Officer but the Public Relations Officer said he didn't know anything about the case and they should go back to Commissioner Quow. After a long wait, Quow met with the mother, assured her the death had been an accident, that her son had kicked an officer, a gun fell to the ground, her son jumped to get it, a scuffle followed and her son got shot.

"I want them to know," Browne's mother told the press, "it's a big nancy story that cannot even be fed to a two year old child." She complained that no one had been allowed to witness the autopsy and that attempts had been made to bury the dead man without the family's knowledge. "One woman cry is all woman cry, it's a nation cry. It is very disturbing for a small country like this."

At the funeral, Pastor David Hunte declared, "David Browne was murdered. It is time to forget political and religious affiliation and stand together." And Pastor Conrad Sayers told the mourners, "We are living in a society where the poor and helpless have become prey to the strong and powerful."

Rastas do not attend funerals but Oba organized brothers of the Nyahbinghi order to join members of the Twelve Tribes,

David Browne's "house," on the streets of "Liberation Square" where they drummed and chanted together through the week to protest the killing and to demand a public inquiry.

In the newspapers following the funeral, the Browne family posted this acknowledgement: "The family of David Browne, July 15,1964–March 9, 2000, would like to convey sincere thanks and appreciation to all those who telephoned, visited, sent cards, wreaths, prayed, offered kind words of sympathy and expressed condolences or in any other way sympathized with us during our recent bereavement. Special thanks to Oba and the members of the Rastafarian Community, Hon. Arnhim Eustace and Mr. Victor Cuffy for their show of solidarity and support."

Long months later, the Commission appointed to investigate the case declared that Browne's death had been an accident.

Drug Wars

In the year 2000, Cecil Blazer Williams, a St.Vincentian historian and journalist, reflected on Browne's death and the rising protests against police behavior in one of the local newspapers. He recalled Haiti under Duvalier and the Ton Ton Macoutes when the rule of law disintegrated and a military dictatorship ruled. "The training (of police) appears to be militaristic in nature with the use of guns being the number one focus. This is dangerous to the peace and stability of the country. Certainly, we do not expect the police to play doll house with hardened criminals but one gets the impression that the use of brute force and other methods which violate the constitutional rights of the citizen have taken hold of a certain section of the police force."

Oba agrees with Williams but presses the analysis to extend beyond the local police force so that it includes the general militarization of the Caribbean occurring as the United States extends its military reach over the region through its War on Drugs. Where Williams writes that the use of brute force has "taken hold of a certain section of the police force," Oba points directly at the "Special Services Unit" which was established in 1984 to control riots and fight drugs.

The English speaking islands of the Eastern Caribbean had moved conspicuously to the "right" in the 1980's because, as Vere Bird, Prime Minister of Antigua put it, "We cannot afford another Cuba or another Grenada." As a result, new agreements were reached with the United States on regional security that called for the prompt initiation of training programs for "Special Services Units" in the islands. United States military aid to the Caribbean soared from 1.2 million dollars in 1982 to 8.5 million in 1985.

James Ferguson traced the important history of those "Special Service Units" back to 1974, the year the United States

Congress passed the Foreign Assistance Act which prohibited the training of foreign "police" by the United States. Not to be thwarted by a word, United States officials sponsored new legislation for "arming and training the para-military Special Services Units which, for the sake of Congress, are defined as 'militias' rather than 'police.'" U.S.Green Beret teams were thus able to begin 6-week training cycles for Caribbean "militias" or "Special Service Units" using the latest in weapons and technology: M-16 rifles, submachine guns, rocket and grenade launchers, telecom and radio systems, uniforms and armored systems.[19]

Ferguson goes on to report that after the Grenada Revolution ended, the ruling parties of that country joined by St. Vincent, St. Lucia, Dominica, Jamaica, Monserrat, St. Kitts-Nevis and Belize met in 1986 to form the Caribbean Democratic Union, an arm of the Worldwide International Democrats founded by Reagan and Thatcher. In that year, the elected leaders of these Caribbean countries gave their enthusiastic support to the political and economic plans the United States had for the region. New defense systems followed immediately and Special Service Units were trained by the United States to prosecute a "war on drugs" as independent Caribbean nations, former colonies of England, sought shelter beneath other wings.

The world-wide reach and influence of the United States' military training programs is nicely illustrated by the fact that the President of Gambia, His Excellency Yahya Jammeh, who came to power after a military coup and whom Oba welcomed to St. Vincent in the name of Africa's scattered sons and daughters, is himself a product of the U.S. Military. According to Gambia's official website, Jammeh was born in 1965, joined the Gambian national police force at the age of 19, transferred to the Gambian army soon after and was a member of the Military Police when the army seized power in 1994. In that year, the future President of Gambia flew to Alabama in the United States and earned a "Diploma in Military Science" at Fort McClellan. He is now not only an African President but an honorary citizen of the state of Georgia and an honorary Lieutenant Colonel of the Alabama State Militia.

Oba argues that the police in the Vincentian Special Services Unit, those trained by the United States and responsible for the island's version of a war on drugs, are the primary source of St.Vincent's "police problem." They are, in his opinion, consistently the most brutal and irresponsible elements on the force and constitute a near-equivalent of a Central American "death squad."

What then does Oba, a man with impressive knowledge of the drug trade, think about the war on drugs itself? When asked, he responds, "What war?" This from a man who knows many of those who grow the crop as well as the boatmen who carry it to market. He estimates that the cultivation of marijuana involves more than 10,000 people in St. Vincent or 10% of population and knows that many more are involved in cleaning and distribution.

Two facts are important here: First, Oba is a Rastafarian who smokes marijuana every day and does so knowing that the holy herb facilitates communion with the Most High. He believes not only that its use should be legalized but that the powerful St. Vincentian weed should become the crop of preference for the island, its niche in the international economy and the key to the island's development and prosperity.

Second, Oba is opposed to hard drugs. He is pleased anytime marijuana can be shared with others because it is a health-giving plant but cocaine and heroin are death-dealing and he will have nothing to do with them. In New York he worked actively with "Black Men Against Crack" and is deeply troubled by the rapid rise in cocaine use on the island and by the violence and corruption associated with its transport and sale. He refuses to be involved in the trade but has friends in all quarters and knows a great deal about it.

The war on drugs in St. Vincent, he believes, comes down to this: an occasional massive assault by the Special Services Unit assisted by USA operated Blackhawk helicopters on small, relatively poor marijuana farmers who watch their income, sheds and plants go up in flames. And what will they do as soon as the smoke clears? They will grow more marijuana. They will cut more trees, clear more land, plant more ganja, and be selling a new crop to the same dependable, well known customers and distributors within six months.

And while Special Services Units sack the countryside and harass small growers, Rastas, and recreational users of grass, planes and ships of all sizes and destinations are moving Colombian cocaine and marijuana in, through, around and out of the island in mountainous quantities. At night bales of Colombian produce are dropped in quiet waters off western shores where men in small boats watch and wait. Colombian boats arrive directly from South America carrying precious freight and heavy arms in case small island coast guard units lose their minds and try to board them. Less than a mile down the road from Oba's home, speedboats come and go with white cargo and Oba's experience with sailing ships suggests that very few yachts are not involved in small or large ways. Yachties make good carriers because they're usually white and move more freely than island boats that have black men at the wheel. And on those huge cruise ships floating leisurely in and out of Caribbean ports with thousands of passengers out for a good time in the tropics, there's an enormous demand for crack and grass which crew members linked to local distribution networks are pleased to satisfy.

Corruption, of course, goes hand in hand with the trade. Drug lords need vassals pledged to look the other way and they find them with ease in places high and low.

The problem is that even if all current vassals of drug lords were exposed and jailed, it would not affect in the least the fundamental dynamics of production, distribution, sale, and use of drugs because there's no shortage of people eager to replace them. Oba sees no evidence for the existence of a real war on drugs or the possibility of winning such a war if one were initiated. He sees, instead, the United States "expanding its military grip and political dominance throughout the region in the name of such a war" and cites recent developments on Union Island as an illustration.

On Jan 18, 2001, "The Herald" of St. Vincent reported that personnel from the United States 7th Naval Mobile Construction Battalion and the US Marine Corp were in St. Vincent and the Grenadines to construct a coast guard sub-base at Clifton, Union Island.

On February 2, 2001, "The Vincentian" newspaper carried a photograph of "US Military Officers at work on the new coast guard sub-base on Union Island" on its front page. In the same issue, the Manager of the Tobago Cays Marine Park, Kurt Cordice, objected that "the process towards the approval of this project has been clouded in mystery" and that the dredging would affect all marine life in the area, including "the loss of precious mangroves, seagrass, coral and particularly young fish." Cordice and other environmentalists wanted and expected a chance to express their serious objections to the project but Prime Minister Mitchell didn't want to hear it, pushed the agreement through, waved off all claims about environmental damage, said the reef was already dead, and announced that the construction would continue and that nobody was going to stop it.

Oba contends that behind the publicity fog it is clear as day that the United States has a new military base on Union Island and will use it for its own purposes, one of which, given its experience with Cuba and Grenada, is to exercise absolute control over the region. The enormous quantities of cocaine now moving through the eastern Caribbean en route to the United States and Europe will continue, now protected by powerful elements within the US military who control surveillance in the islands. Police and politicians will prosper from the payoffs, small dealers will be hassled and get desperate, guns and crime will increase, and only a handful of Vincentians will see the connections and protest.

In 2003, two years after the Unity Labor Party took political power in St. Vincent, Oba reports that the police campaign against marijuana production and trafficking is more vigorous than ever but that raids on small, local users like Oba have been radically reduced. He and other Rastas now feel far more secure in their homes, fairly confident that heavily armed policemen are not going to come in the night to raid and plant evidence against them.

Oba continues to believe that St. Vincent should begin to act like the independent nation it's supposed to be and legalize marijuana so that all who want to use it can enjoy its blessings and the country can reap the economic benefits of an internationally popular crop. Bananas, he argues, have run their course not only because the island is losing preferential market agreements with Europeans but also because the pesticides used in banana production have depleted natural microorganisms and destroyed the once fertile soil.

7

Rastas, Politics and St. Vincent's Future

> *. . . even when there were not great leaders present, the mass of people have constantly been acting against the system. In our epoch the Rastafari have represented the leading force of this expression of black consciousness. They have rejected the philistine, white West Indian society. They have sought their cultural and spiritual roots in Ethiopia and Africa. So that whether there is a big flare up or not, there is always the constant activity of the black people who perceive that the system has nothing in it for them except suppression and oppression.*
>
> Walter Rodney, *Groundings with My Brothers*

+

On a clear day in the spring of the year 2000, Oba stood in the middle of the highway above the Vincentian airport watching the police coming toward him. Their orders were to clear the road of protesters, trees, buses, anyone and anything snarling traffic. Oba raised his bullhorn, called to the men and women blocking cars to stand their ground, assured them that all major roads to the city had been closed, the blockade was working, the great majority of Vincentians were behind them, and now was the time to stay united against the self-serving government of Prime Minister James Mitchell.

The police paused long enough to challenge Oba's right to use a bullhorn and swept on past him. Their sights were on Ralph Gonsalves, leader of the Unity Labor Party and organizer of the massive protest that was closing the country down. They found Gonsalves in a car at the blockade's command center but as they moved toward him, hundreds of Vincentians formed a human shield around "the Comrade" and refused to move. The police, challenged, outnumbered and uncertain, backed off slowly and moved away.

What was going on? Briefly this: the Parliament controlled by the party of Prime Minister Mitchell had denied salary increases to school teachers, nurses and other government workers because there was no money in the treasury but at the same time passed a "Pensions and Gratuities Bill" that granted salary and pension increases to themselves. The Unity Labor Party led by Gonsalves opposed the bill and joined the unions and other organizations of the country in protests to force retraction of the measure. A new "Organization in Defense of Democracy," broadly representative of civil society with schoolteachers, nurses, and government workers in the lead was formed and the decision made to close St. Vincent down.

The country was soon paralyzed. Leaders of other Caribbean nations watched the unfolding events anxiously, not excited by the idea that a popular uprising was being used to overturn decisions made by a legally constituted Parliament. Representatives of the Caribbean Community, CARICOM, flew into St. Vincent to facilitate negotiations. Dr. Ralph Gonsalves, leader of the organized opposition and his party's candidate to lead the country as Prime Minister, demanded early elections so the people could decide which party best represented their interests. In the end, Gonsalves won, Mitchell lost. Elections were to be held no later than March, 2001.

Tim Hector, a major Caribbean intellectual and activist, believed those actions to be among the most important in the history of the English speaking Caribbean because they illustrated the peoples' desire and capacity for direct participation in their own governance rather than relinquishing such participation as soon as an election is concluded.

Hector's views in the year 2000 were entirely consistent with his convictions as a young man studying with C.L.R. James in the 1960s. During those early years he and other Caribbean students at Sir George Williams University in Canada dedicated themselves to return to their home islands and advance "radical democracy" by which they meant the organization of people not just to vote but to govern in village and town through councils enabling them to discuss initiatives proposed by Parliament, to propose new initiatives, and with "their own self-government" replace the remaining power of the state and fashion a new and unparalleled democracy.

Oba knew Hector's work well and believed no one was better qualified to interpret the importance of the protests and the results that became known as the "Grand Beach Accords."

Hector wrote that although Caribbean newspapers had paid scant attention to the Vincentian protests, he believed they represented "the most momentous event to take place in the English speaking Caribbean since these island-states gained independence" because they represented "a mass movement, not equalling in numbers, but surpassing the mass movement in Trinidad in 1970 in terms of political clarity of purpose" and actually forced the government to hold early elections.

The event, he wrote, "bespeaks a new mass democratic impulse. It is a most stunning development. People organizing themselves in the English-speaking Caribbean and bringing a duly elected government to a halt. Demanding redress of their grievances. And when government seemed heedless of the governed, the governed made the government take heed. The St. Vincent crisis, or if you prefer, the St. Vincent rebellion, is not the culmination, it is a continuation of a crisis between government and the governed in the entire Caribbean. People no longer wish to be governed in the old way. It is a thorough-going crisis. I shall be even more specific. People do not wish to be represented. They wish to represent themselves, through various organs which are firmly in their social control. Government of the people, by the people, must mean exactly what it says, of the people and by the people.

"What is beyond doubt is that the battle lines are drawn. The coming period of Caribbean history will see these mass challenges to a political system which locks out people, except for a vote every five years. People will open these locked systems and create new organs for the management of society, for themselves, of themselves, by themselves." [20]

Oba agrees with Hector on the importance of organizing local, democratic councils to not only monitor the actions of elected official but also to increase the direct self-government of the people in all areas possible. So once elections were assured, Oba worked closely with Spirit Cottle, Chairman of the United Front for Progress, to secure as much Rasta and Dread support for the Gonsalves' led Unity Labor Party as possible. They drafted and addressed a letter to all "Rastafarians and Dreads," a letter important for what it reveals about the long experience of Rastas and Dreads in St. Vincent and for the new, united turn toward political engagement it may represent.

The letter began, "This is a crucial time in the history of our nation. It is also a very significant one for Rastafarians and Dreads because with all the wickedness you have been facing in the country, with all the police brutality and killings of Rastafarians and Dreadlocks brethren, especially under the New Democratic Party government of James Mitchell and Arnhim Eustance, the political opportunity has never been better to 'big up' Rastafarians and Dreads in this country. . . . The choice will be between three political parties, the People's Progressive Movement, the New Democratic Party, and the Unity Labor Party. . . . the PPM hasn't got much to offer and even though it has a Rasta as one of its candidates, that brother has no connection with the movement of Rasafarians."

The letter reminded Rastas and Dreads that Mitchell and the New Democratic Party had been in power for 16 years and "our brothers and sisters have never suffered as much under a government as they have under the NDP, and no other government hands have been stained with the blood of Rastafarians and Dreads as the governments of James Mitchell and Arnhim Eustace. . . . Rastafarians and Dreads are from the poorer classes of society, we suffer because we are poor, and unless we are an integral part of the struggle of poor people, unless we are part of the larger movement of the majority of our people against those who oppress and exploit us all, we as Rastafarians and Dreads shall never be able to bring the discrimination against us to an end and gain the respect we deserve. The Unity Labor Party and Comrade Ralph has been the only political party and leader respectively who have offered the Rastafarian and Dreadlocks Brethren and Sisteren this opportunity. . . ."

Significant numbers of Rastafarians in St. Vincent, however, wanted nothing to do with any political party and branded those involved as "sell-outs" because, they argued, the way of the Rasta is the way of separation from the forms and seductions of Babylon and the false hope that political activity will lead to justice for the poor or righteousness in the eyes of Jah Rastafari.

Oba, on the other hand, insisted that Rastas should be powerful advocates for the poor and the oppressed in national and international forums and that such advocacy required organization and independent political activity at many levels. Although the redemption of the world would come when and only when the Almighty initiates His Divine theocracy, political action is necessary in order to secure some measure of relief for suffering people now.

Clear precedents for political activity by Rastafarians exist. In 1958, "The Star" of Jamaica reported that "The city of Kingston was 'captured' near dawn on Saturday by some 300 bearded men of the Rastafarian cult along with their women and children. About 3:30 AM early market-goers saw members of the Rastafarian movement gathered in the center of Victoria Park with towering poles, atop of which, fluttered black, green, and red banners, loudly proclaiming that they had captured the city. . . . When the police moved toward them, a leader of the group with his hands raised issued a warning to the police: touch not the Lord's annointed." [21]

A leading Rastafarian elder, Sam Brown, ran for public office in Jamaica in 1961. During the campaign, Brown explained that the Rastafarian movement had been subject to persecution and discrimination and had given its support to the major parties but gotten little or nothing for their efforts. They had therefore decided to create a political movement with the aim of taking power and implementing measures for the uplift of the poor and oppressed. The campaign did not go well. Brown gained all of one hundred votes. [22]

The Rastas of St. Vincent have generally kept their distance from politics but the election of 2001 may have marked the beginning of an important shift because several leading Rastas were vigorously partisan during the election. Oba worked for a Unity Labor Party victory, another prominent Rasta hosted a daily radio program promoting the New Democratic Party while a third was a candidate for the Peoples' Progressive Movement.

All this political activity did not go unnoticed by Rastas from Grenada, Barbados and Trinidad, long time friends of Oba's who had come to visit and promote a film advocating the legalization of marijuana. Orthodox Nyahbinghi in the tradition of Ras Boanerges, they were troubled by Oba's participation in the campaign and reminded him that a Rasta's confidence should be in the Most High and not in political power. His energies, they insisted, should be given instead to the work of repatriation to Africa or to the Rasta efforts in Panama.

"At one time," Oba says, "I took the same position but now I believe we're responsible to at least vote." To him, Gonsalves and the Unity Labor Party represented something new in Vincentian politics, some possibility for change in the lives of poor people, and he threw himself into the campaign. At the same time, he did not believe that Rastas as a group should endorse a candidate. Advocacy of particular parties and candidates should remain the prerogative of individual Rastas and no attempt should be made to get the Rasta community as a whole to take a partisan position.

When the people finally voted, the results were overwhelming. The Unity Labor Party won 12 of 15 parliamentary seats, Ralph Gonsalves became the new Prime Minister of St. Vincent and initiated what Rastas and Dreads hope to be a new day in the eastern Caribbean.

The best intentions to reduce poverty and unemployment in a small Caribbean nation are, of course, countered by stubborn problems. These are, as Gonsalves sees them, severely limited geographical space and physical resources, small populations, susceptibility to natural disasters, fragile ecological systems, underdeveloped economies, a shortage of highly skilled manpower, economic dependence on one or two export goods or services, and political marginalization in the post-Cold War world.

At the same time, he points out that his country enjoys a fifty year history of stable, democratic governance; a young, trained and trainable population; a location and physical assets attractive to tourists and offshore finance centers; an influential population in the diaspora; and human development indices "not wholly unmeritorious" as St. Vincent is ranked 75th among 174 countries of the world by the United Nations' Human Development Report of 1999 compared to a rating of 29 for Barbados, 46 for Trinidad and Tobago, 52 for Grenada, and 152 for Haiti. [23]

Given these conditions, how can St. Vincent best provide the employment and income necessary for a decent standard of living among its people?

Historically, agriculture has been the answer. But as Vincentian historian Edgar Adams has documented, over the long years one after another of St. Vincent's crops has declined in value: sugar, sea island cotton, arrowroot, and now bananas. Adams agrees with the judgment of C.I. Martin, "The Commonwealth Caribbean has so far found it difficult if not impossible to produce agricultural commodities under competitive conditions. Indeed the survival of particular crop industries has, for the most part, depended on one of two conditions: either the product has been accorded preferential treatment in the metropolitan countries or the producing territory has a monopoly on the production of the particular crop. The commodities which have been accorded preferential treatment (sugar, bananas) play a much greater role in Caribbean economies than those that were produced under monopoly conditions (arrowroot, nutmeg, pimiento, sea island cotton)."[24]

In the late 1990s, then Prime Minister Mitchell made it clear that St. Vincent's economic base had shifted dramatically from bananas to tourism. Income from bananas, St. Vincent's primary crop since the 1950s, peaked in 1992 at 102 million dollars but fell to 37 million by 1997. At the same time, tourism was on the rise with 114,000 visitors in 1984 and 202,000 in 1998. The tourist industry, once providing only half the revenue obtained from banana sales now brought to the island four times as much as the once favored fruit. The preferential trading agreements St. Vincent and other former colonies enjoyed with Britain had been challenged by the World Trade Organization and there was general agreement that a new period in the island's economic history had begun.

The decline of agriculture and the limited prospects for small manufacturers have led St. Vincent and all other islands to cast about for options. Off-shore financial centers have been established but these run into problems with the Organization for Economic Cooperation and Development which accuses nations like St. Vincent of "encouraging tax evasion" and threatens economic sanctions. And, of course, computers make it possible for businesses to use "in-put service centers" located anywhere in the world and St. Vincent has expressed interest in being involved.

But it is tourism, the world's largest and fastest growing industry, on which most islands are placing their best hopes. Every island is involved in the business and most are dependent on it. In his 1999 Independence Day address, then Prime Minister Mitchell tied St. Vincent's economic future firmly not only to tourism but tourism for the rich. His dream was "a quality of development along our Leeward coast that matches the elegance of any sophisticated Riviera in the world with our picturesque inlets matching the class of Porto Fino. Our millennium Cruise Berth will be opened during November. The luxurious Canouan Resort with 178 rooms and an 18 hole, 72 par spectacular golf course and casino will be opened in December."

The "luxurious Canouan Resort" of Mitchell's dreams did open and was the site for a meeting of Caribbean leaders in the year 2000. Speaking to his political peers on that occasion, Mitchell recalled with pleasure that the elegant, "world class" resort they were all so enjoying had, only a few years ago, been the location for "jungle training exercises by the Regional Security System" and said the multi-million dollar resort showed how tourism can be used to meet the challenges of globalization.

Exactly how another playground for the rich meets the challenges of globalization is not explained. Construction of a luxurious resort may, importantly, provide a few jobs for Vincentians but it "meets" none of the serious economic and cultural challenges of globalization. On the contrary, in most cases it simply extends the reach of foreign, unregulated capital into another corner of the impoverished globe where a compliant government lures investors with promises of tax and infrastructural benefits along with an able but unorganized workforce.

The Carenage Bay Beach Resort and Golf Club about which Mitchell spoke rents villa suites with 100% Frette cotton terry bath towels, feather pillows, twice daily housekeeping, computer connections, and satellite television for between $450 and $1200 a night plus tax and service charges. The accompanying pleasures include an 18-hole golf course, European casinos, tennis, yachts, scuba, one of the Caribbean's largest fresh water pools and so forth. The island itself is arid and short of water. The new resort has its own seawater desalinization plant and never runs dry.

The Resorts' neighbors on Canouan are a thousand Vincentians, people traditionally involved in fishing and farming. Small resorts have been on the island for years but the

Carenage Bay Beach Resort and Golf Club is what folks mean when they talk about "The Resort" because it now dominates the island physically and economically. By agreement with the government of St. Vincent and the Grenadines, the Resort has a 99 year lease giving it control over 3/4 of the island or 1200 of its 1866 acres.

Those living on Canouan generally welcomed the resort's development because it provided work during construction, the promise of regular employment when completed, and a new market for island farmers and fishermen.

Conflicts emerged, however, over the use of the beaches on the resort's land. Vincentians had used those beaches all their lives and assumed they'd continue to do so. It was still their island, wasn't it? The Resort, on the other hand, had created a space whose charm and profits depended considerably on its exclusive, peaceful, untroubled, hassle-free character and therefore closed "its" beaches to locals.

Residents of Canouan responded by blocking the roads in and out of the resort. Police and politicians were immediately involved and in the spring of 2001, a court order gave the people of Canouan rights to the contested beach. Reports, however, continued to circulate that access was being denied by The Resort's guards.

In the meantime, American Airlines suspended flights to St. Vincent but initiated four weekly flights to tiny Canouan while the resort's managers in Texas spread word on worldwide, upscale golfing circuits that a new posh place had surfaced in the Eastern Caribbean. Somewhat dramatically, airline maps of the Caribbean were also changed. In those contained within American Airlines' flight magazines, St. Vincent is no longer to be found. The only island between Grenada and St. Lucia given a name is now Canouan.

Bananas failing, luxury tourism in the ascendancy, persistent poverty and unemployment the lot of too many Vincentians. How will the new, Gonsalves led government approach the nation's problems?

An early leader of socialist formations on the island in the 1970s, Gonsalves writes in these later, very different years that "I have been searching in the aftermath of the failed gods of centrally planned regimes, on the one hand, and of unbridled capitalism/neo-liberalism on the other for an overarching framework from which to draw solutions." He has come to believe that in the present period, "the fashioning of a mixed economy and a deepening democratic political system provide the best framework for the fulsome linking of freedom, equality, economic justice, increased productivity and economic efficiency. We thus say 'yes' to a market economy with regulation, but 'no' to a market society." [25]

He also quotes with approval the perspective of Will Hutton, author of *The State to Come*, "One lesson of our times may be that capitalism has triumphed for the moment in the great battle with socialism . . . . But the moral and religious values which informed the socialist and social democratic movements of the twentieth century along with their fierce advocacy of liberty, cannot be consigned to history without endangering the civilization which we prize. Another lesson of our times is surely that the operation of the unchecked market, whatever its success in sending effective messages about what is scarce and what is abundant, has an inherent tendency to produce unreasonable inequality, economic instability and immense concentrations of private, unaccountable power. To protect itself, society has to have countervailing powers built into the operation of the market, otherwise the market cannot deliver its promise. Instead it collapses into license masquerading as liberty, spivvery dressed up as risk-taking and exploitation in the guise of efficiency and flexibility."[26]

There is, as one might expect, no uniform Rasta perspective on the social and economic development of the island and no intent to form one. Most Rastas go their own unaffiliated way and neither the Nyahbinghi, the Twelve Tribes or the Bobo Dread make pronouncements on these matters.

There are, however, convictions common to Vincentian Rastas which cause them to value some directions more than others. Their love of the "natural," their fierce rejection of Babylon and their desire to be free and independent of its lures incline them toward self-sufficiency, agriculture and food. In St. Vincent, the great majority of its 3000 to 4000 Rastafarians are small farmers committed to agriculture as their preferred way of life. And they insist that agriculture should not, cannot be shrugged off as a thing of the past simply because bananas no longer make it on international markets. In any and all conversations about the way forward for the country, it is on this issue of economic development and growth that Oba and other Rastas most clearly separate themselves from prevailing cultural expectations and definitions of progress.

Over the last hundred years, the people of the world have moved steadily off the land and into cities in pursuit of a better life. Rastas are one of the counter-currents. They remain at every point in the food chain on the main island of St. Vincent and on the smaller islands of Bequia and the Grenadines they pretty much control the process. They want to farm and believe small farming to be the natural way for Rastas to assure their food supply. Oba says, "We not only farm but we eat what we produce. We want to eat proper and organic and therefore we've got to control the process. I want to sustain myself and control production of my family's food so we can be healthy."

G.A. Griffin, reflecting on the impact of luxury tourism on Nevis, the small Caribbean island of his birth, wrote,

"Long before the advent of the golf plantation, small-scale subsistence farming was a vital means of physical, cultural, and psychological survival. . . . To stave off starvation, we farmed the land . . . and developed a whole complex of socio-economic relations that became a fundamental basis of the Afro-Caribbean community. Farming gave slaves a foothold from which to maintain their cultural and social presence in a society after they had been entirely marginalized. If the subsistence wages paid by (a resort) have lured Nevisians away from the practical and symbolic power of working for themselves, it has done more than slavery could."[27]

Turning their backs on Babylon, Rastas have turned their backs on the accumulation of commodities as the measure of a life's worth. Money for light in the house and gas for the stove are good things but material possessions don't really count for much in their catalogue of riches. They've committed themselves instead to a life of "I and I" relations of peace and respect with all beings, strong families, and the tradition of small farming. They believe this to be a forward and not a backward move. It is modern society that has taken a wrong turn away from the natural.

Oba argues that the nation should be moving toward more, not less agriculture. An agro-army of the youth of the nation could and should be organized because there are no opportunities for the young and for lack of options they get pressed into the drug trade. "An agro-army of organic farmers could be organized from the youth of the land. Do it along cooperative lines. Give the youth life-saving skills, teach them farming and an independent kind of life." He rejects the idea that young men and women are no longer willing to work the land and is sure that if given the opportunity to make their work productive, the youth of the nation would be immediately interested.

He takes an article from Newsweek, February 26, 2001, out of his pocket and reads a report on the growing demand for organic produce in England, such a demand "that the nation's second largest grocery chain, Sainsbury's, is working to realize the goal of a totally organic island in the Caribbean. It is discussing an agreement in the Windward Islands with Grenada, Dominica, St. Lucia, and St. Vincent to produce organic bananas, mangoes, coconuts, and other fruits for a 'guaranteed' British market." Properly supported and planned, Oba says, the expansion of organic farming would be important not just to Rastas and other farmers but to the nation as a whole because the demand for organic food is going to keep on growing.

Apart from or along with work as small farmers, most St. Vincent Rastas, who today have a level of education that did not exist in the seventies, are also carpenters and construction workers, tradesmen, artists, and small entrepreneurs buying and selling food and other products. In early 2003, for example, Oba was working as a security guard by night and tending crops in his yard by day.

He and other Rastas tend not to be strongly opposed to any of the possibilities proposed for economic development but they put their own interpretation on them. Say "tourism" to Oba and his immediate response is not a negative blast about the cultural distortions implicit in the business but a positive word for eco-tourism. "Taking care of trails, showing people waterfalls, hiking in the mountains, going up the volcano, man, that's the kind of thing we love to do. That's the way we lived in the early days, up in the mountains, cooking, sleeping outside."

Say "business" and he tells you the Nyahbinghi are going to initiate a cooperative trade with other islands and Caribbean countries. "We're going to get a boat together, sell food in Barbados, import special oils and coal from Guyana. They produce coal from wood down there so hard it burns blue." He also believes it's only a matter of time until people on the island will be able to grow and sell marijuana for medical and industrial purposes.

8

"We Forward . . . Triumphantly"

Ole pirates yes they rob I

Sold I to the merchant ships

Minutes after they took I

From the bottomless pits

But my hands were made strong

By the hands of the Almighty

We forward in this generation

Triumphantly

–Bob Marley

The enormous social distance traveled by the Rastas of St. Vincent since their emergence on the island in the 1970s was dramatized in 2003 by an article in "Focus," a publication of the St. Vincent government. The report, entitled "Prime Minister Meets With Rastafarians," was accompanied by a large photograph of Dr. Gonsalves and the Rasta brethren, Oba clearly visible among them, seated at a common table. The discussions, described as "very positive," focused on repatriation, increased diplomatic and cultural ties to Ethiopia, Rasta participation in regional trade, and human rights education in the schools.

Thirty years ago, the only branch of government interested in contact with Rastas was the police department. Today they sit with a sympathetic Prime Minister and discuss common concerns.

Oba sees these changes as part of a decisive Nyahbinghi turn toward health and strength. "We have a new Priest, a new tabernacle and we're maintaining our livity. We're not selling out, we're rejuvenating. St. Vincent's now looked on as a powerhouse for the Nyahbinghi. We're building an economic base, we're keeping a balance in the King's treasury and we're much more solid now."

Rasta Convictions: Continuity and Change

And have Rasta beliefs also changed, grown stronger? Oba looked over a list of six basic convictions identified as "uniquely Rastafarian" by Leonard Barrett, a pioneer in Rasta studies since the 1960s, and talked about them.[28]

1. Haile Selassie is the living God.

Oba affirms this as the continuing central conviction of Rastafarians.

"If, as you say, Haile Selassie is the Christman in his second coming as King of King, Lord of Lords, Conquering Lion of the Tribe of Judah, what's the difference between His Imperial Majesty Haile Selassie, Jesus and God?"

"They're actually one and the same. 2000 years ago Jesus the Christman came as the lamb and was crucified for our sins. He told us there would be another, a second and final coming of the Christman but not as the lamb. In the second dispensation he comes as the lion of the tribe of Judah. That has now happened in Haile Selassie, King of King and Lord of Lords."

Dr. Rex Nettleford, Chancellor at the University of the West Indies, and a scholar close to the Rastafarian movement, adds his own useful reflections on the Rasta affirmation of a black God, "The Rastafarians have tuned into a major strategy of demarginalization: religion. Having one's own God in one's own image was a grand flowering in Rastafari of what had earlier begun in Myal and developed in Zion Revivalism and Pocomania, with the hijacking of the oppressor's God in a move that served to discommode the oppressor. The slave forbears of Rastafarians understood fully that there are areas of inviolability beyond the reach of oppressors, and that these are what guarantee survival and beyond. Such exercise of the creative imagination and intellect remains, then, the most powerful weapon against all acts of inhumanity."[29]

2. The Black person is the reincarnation of ancient Israel, who, at the hand of the white person, has been in exile in Jamaica.

"Yes, the Bible is the black man's history rewritten and distorted by Europeans who made it into a white man's book. If whites insist on dividing people into one of two colors, blacks or white, then Jesus was certainly a black man and the Israelites were black people. The Bible doesn't just tell the story of some oppressed people who suffered in ancient times the way black people suffer now. The Bible tells the story of black people then and black people now."

3.The white person is inferior to the black person.

"For myself, I don't think that holds true right across the board. I've seen an opening up of not being so anti-white. That kind of reverse reaction is not so common anymore. All that changed for me in Vermont where the white community was extremely supportive. I think all men and women are called to participate in the Divine Life. We all belong to the human race and have to work out some way to live in harmony. We can't turn anyone away 'cause we don't know what's in a person's heart. And we can't stop anyone from seeing Selassie."

4.The Jamaican situation is a hopeless hell; Ethiopia is heaven.

"Ethiopia could be considered heaven only if Ethiopia means all of Africa, the homeland, transformed by the Divine theocracy to be inaugurated when the Almighty in His good time decides to do so. But in the meantime, yes, we’re determined to return to Africa. Africa’s our focus, our home.”

5. The Invincible Emperor of Ethiopia is now arranging for expatriated persons of African origin to return to Ethiopia.

“No one’s stopping anyone from going right now. There’s land available in Ethiopia, 500 acres dedicated by Selassie I for anyone who wants to come. But we have to be clear, if we have a problem here, that problem is not going away because we move to Africa. My own fulfillment lies in Africa but I need to be equipped mentally and at least have farm implements so that when I land, I can sustain myself. And yes, the power of divinity is at work toward repatriation. If we keep our focus and purify ourselves, all will be manifested.”

6. In the near future blacks shall rule the world.

“I don’t have that in me. I see all as equal and all need to coexist in peace. We can have our own borders with equality between us. None of us get up in the tabernacle and discredit anyone who comes in the name of His Imperial Majesty.”

+

The New Tabernacle

Much of the new strength described by Oba was generated in 2002 during a Nyahbinghi gathering to worship, celebrate Selassie’s visit to the Caribbean in 1966, and make a series of changes in their life together. Night after night, they chanted and drummed and made two key decisions: they chose I Man I to be their new Priest and they decided to build a Tabernacle in Oba's yard.

A new Tabernacle had been needed for years because the previous one had been so contaminated by division, hostility and bitterness that it was worthless as a place for praises and supplications. Following the detailed guidelines used wherever Nyahbinghi gather, they built the Tabernacle themselves with twelve outer posts representing, among others, the 12 tribes of Israel and the Twelve Apostles, The large center post of the Tabernacle represents "I and I Ivine Majesty, Emperor Haile Selassie I who is the Head of the Nyahbinghi Order."

During the twice-weekly services in the Tabernacle, herb is always on the altar as their pure and holy sacrifice to the Most High and two fires burn continually, the judgment fire and the mercy fire. "When we're together," Oba explained, "we call fire down for destruction and purification. When someone chants 'fire' at you, you know you've been eating wrong or gotten involved in carnality, gambling or whoredom and you have to purge yourself because you can't reach Zion with a carnal mind. It's not so accepted among us that you can sin and always be forgiven. We come down real hard on those who backslide. It lights a fire in you. There's an internal fire that can be lit and it helps to purify you. Love, too. For love you send out fire. Fire 'pon de chicken mout! Fire! We throw wood on the judgment fire to burn up sins, to chant down something and bap! it's gone. The mercy fire is where you make your penitence and gain forgiveness."

"Penitence for what?

"Wrong doing, corruption, lying, cheating, basic moral values, being loyal to your spouse, violating truths and rights."

"What's the problem with chicken?"

"We want to get back to our true, pre-slavery being because it's necessary to keep the temple clean and you can't do that without good nutrition. The purer the body, the purer the mind. The purer we are the more open and receptive we are to the Divine. Rastas stay very close to pure, organic food and we grow as much of our own as possible--that's why so many of us are farmers. Flesh, alcohol, cigarettes harm the body, harm the mind, clog up divine channels. In the early days, brothers threw away their knives, forks and steel pots and moved around the countryside carrying a yaba, an unglazed pot never used for cooking flesh."

"You say that being a Rasta gives you strength and confidence because you're now clear about who you are. Who are you?"

"I'm one of the reincarnated souls prior to the holocaust, prior to slavery."

"Reincarnated soul?"

"Yes. Most Rastas might not put it that way but I'm more conscious of my Africanness than my Vincentianness."

"What does redemption mean to you?"

"Redemption from the white world and all those feelings of inferiority they put on you. Redemption means becoming your true self, redeeming your dignity in a hostile world."

"Why 'fear' of the Almighty? Why 'dread'?"

"It's fear of not doing the right thing. There are always consequences to what you do and I see myself as responsible for all my actions. If I get off the path, I'm vulnerable to different forces. I'm weaker."

"The Nyahbinghi creed includes a prayer for the hungry, the naked, the sick, the aged and the infants. Is there any organized effort to provide that care?"

"There's no question we agree about those things and we all share what we have with others. We're known for that. But most Rastas can't do much except at the personal sharing level 'cause they're scrabbling for a living themselves. The majority of Rastas are poor and hard pressed and working all the time. Our Priest, I Man I, he can't miss a day's work if his family's going to have food on the table."

"Marley sang 'we forward in this generation triumphantly.' You feel that way?"

"Yes, triumphantly . . . It's been a great triumph to break with slavery, a triumph to make a clean, clear break with Babylon. The Almighty empowers us."

And as the Nyahbinghi community increases in strength and clarity of purpose, so that community has become more and more central to Oba.

Rasta Men and Rasta Women

Oba has observed that the treatment of women by Rasta men has changed substantially since the seventies. "There was a lot of immature behavior in the past toward women. Now aggressions against women aren't tolerated. We're less dogmatic about a lot of things. More brethren and sistren are going through books and other material by themselves and analyzing things from their own point of view. And it's hard on Rasta women cause we're not the best providers with stable paychecks every week. When I met Dafina she was already locksed up so she didn't become a Rasta because of me. So I see a steady growth in the Nyahbinghi, we're getting more human with each other when in the past there was a lot of screwface among us."

"We denounce domestic violence in all its forms as copycat behavior from the masters," Oba declared. "The African male has some disorders like anyone else and we need to overcome them. We're accused of being chauvinistic but equal conversations between men and women are taking place all the time. The black woman is a tower of strength. They get things done. At a meeting last night a brother said 'yes, we'll do that,' and a sister challenged him, 'Yes but who is 'we,' who exactly is going to do it?' Women have emerged who stand up and face all the dogmas and negativity against women and yet continue to promote the Rasta livity."

"We have different responsibilities. We know that women are especially vulnerable during menstruation and open to spiritual experiences so a man should cook for her at that time and let her focus on herself. There was a time when brothers said a woman menstruating was 'unclean' but we fought that and discourage any disrespect for women. We have to recognize that Rastafari attracts all types and some are more dogmatic than others but everything evolves and people change."

"Would Rasta men chant down one another for having outside women?"

"Not in public but privately, sure. It's a mark of disrespect for your Queen. Our livity's important--we learned a lot from the Muslim community. Malcolm X had a strict code of ethics. You respected women, you supported your children. We've been bad fathers and must accept that fact and change. I know I need a home. I have six kids and I tell you I don't have no bank account. My aim is to become more productive, learn from negative experiences, turn them around.”

One Sunday afternoon, a few Nyahbinghi men gathered in Oba’s home to prepare for the evening’s service. They welcomed me and my interest in them. I asked about the Nyahbinghi rule that women cannot administrate around the altar or prophesy before the congregation. The following responses came from different men and do not represent a consensus among them. I said, “There’s a long African tradition of women leading their communities in spiritual and political matters. So why can’t Rasta women prophesy in the Tabernacle?”

“They can and they do. Whatever my daughter says or wants to say it’s my responsibility to put it on the table, just like if you’re not a member of the UN you have to go through someone who is. I’ll put anything on the table that she’s wants to say.”

“But why does she have to go through you? Your wives are strong, intelligent, hard-working women. You say you’re equal in your home. Why isn’t she equal in the Tabernacle?

“Cause that’s our tradition. There’s no doubt that women are a source of strength for the men but it’s our tradition that keeps us from straying and I’ve never heard any Nyahbinghi woman challenge it. There’s so much confusion in other churches. In some of them a man can even marry a man. How could a person accept that? Remember, when Selassie was coronated, his wife was sitting right beside him, so she wasn't back and he forward. I think it has to do with the zest and the protection of the order which is a lifeline for us. If that order had not been preserved, where would I be now? You're kind of lost in direction but the order's been preserved and that's no coincidence.

"Women can't attend services when menstruating?"

"No, it's a time of cleansing."

"Why do you call a natural process unclean?"

"Cause her body's cleaning out something dead."

"And they're prone to all sorts of influences when menstruating. I can tell when my wife has her period. There are changes."

"She doesn't lose her mind, does she? She doesn't stop being intelligent and strong?"

"No, but she gets moody."

"There's some sense in all this that women are less able than men when it comes to spiritual things. Is that what you think?"

"Yes, yes, I think so."

"And Nyabinghi women aren't bothered by this?

"Look, it's the women who aren't in this movement who are always sticking it to us on this. I don't hear no Nyahbinghi woman raising these issues. I see a white feminist movement trying to co-opt black women. Most black women don't go with the white feminist movement cause black people have a common oppressor."

+

A few days later, I met with three women of the Nyahbinghi order, Sister I Deka, Sister I Land, and Sister Azizza Miyazya.

Sister I Deka had been raised an Anglican, Sister I Land a Methodist, and Sister Azziza Miyazya had felt close to the Pentacostals when she was a teenager. I asked what attracted them to Rastafari.

Sister I Deka: "Really and truly, within these churches you don't find the spirit I was looking for. To be frank with you, from the time I was a little girl I was always interested in the Rastafari movement. As I got older I began to see the brethren and sistren and the way they trod. I was attracted by Rasta naturalness, natural living, and had always been looking for that kind of livity. As a child our church had a crusade. It was an altar call and I went up because I was looking for something more than what I was getting in the Anglican church, but eventually I was still not satisfied with the spiritual life until I had my first child at age 16 and then I met my husband who was a Rasta and from then with strength from him and others I was in the faith until today."

Sister I Land: "As a young woman I got the opportunity to go to Yulimo, a black movement organization and I learned more about black history and culture. From then on I was fighting for blackness until a Rasta man show me about His Majesty and even more about Africa and by doing so I move on to the Rasta."

Sister Azizza Miyazya: "As a teenager I felt close to the Pentecostals but my mother was conscious about her blackness so because of that particular gift from my mother I had the urging to learn more about the Bible and black people so I started searching and finally connected to Rastafari as a culture and as a people who uplift blackness as the key objective. Basically we see a black King, we identify black people as founding fathers of firstly Christianity and other so called mighty things that we have in this society. So Rastafari taught me all the things I need to know and filled a gap that I wanted to be filled as a black person. It made it clear for me and so I naturally grew in that direction."

"Why can't women prophesy in the tabernacle?"

"We do prophesy only not at the altar because that is where there's a great power and the Priest administrates. It may look to the eyes like something physical but there's universal power there and that power was given to the Kings to administrate."

"Because men are superior spiritually?"

I Deka: "No, I wouldn't say that. That's their portion—to administrate"

Azziza, "You must have limitations because of the makeup of a woman. But there are limitations on man too. The daughter has the same power to relate to the Creator as the man. She is not less."

"Limited because of her menstrual cycle?"

I Deka: "Partly, but not totally. From the beginning, that portion of the work, prophecy, was given to the high priest. It's the tradition and certain things in the tradition cannot be changed. As Christ is head of the church, so the man is head of the house."

"What do you say to those who respond, 'Yes, traditionally the man has been head of the house and that's the problem. Women had the same powers to prophesy, women were equally intelligent, women worked as hard but men had the power to shape the tradition and shaped it to serve themselves.'"

I Deka: "There's no compromising righteousness. What has already been set and said, that cannot be changed. Certain things like the administration is not to be changed."

Azizza Miyaza: "That kind of attitude on a woman's part, feeling like she's less a person because traditionally it's said that man is ruler of the home, that kind of thinking may be how the man might portray himself but a man don't have to go around with I a man and I the ruler because at home we relate, we share ideas, we communicate. One thing I must commend our Rastaman I for is he never keep down his woman, he never say well I over you because I am at the altar doing whatever. We relate, we have children, we have to work together to have them grow up to be good people to show forth to their children the principles. So it is not to say that I am over you or under you, just that we all work together."

Maureen Rowe, a Jamaican Rasta and educator, sorted through many of these issues with her sisters. "I have been asked on more than one occasion why the Rastafari sistren have not openly challenged the restrictions of the movement. Why, for example, have not a group of females decided to stand up together and reason in the tabernacle? I can only speculate in answer to these questions. What I have observed of the women in the movement is a protectiveness of the movement itself. Recognizing that Babylon was hostile to everything that Rastafari stood for, the women were unlikely to mount the kind of challenge that could contribute to the destruction of the movement from within."[30]

And Imani M.Tafari-Ama adds, "What is clear is that the contradictions of race, class, and gender distinctions operate as beguilingly in Rastafari as they do in the wider society. . . . to a great extent, patriarchal emphases in Rastafari are due to the translation into the livity of practices and beliefs derived from ancient Israel and Christianity.. . .that is, Rastafari does not present a unique example of the manifestation of patriarchy."[31]

Repatriation

From their first years in bondage, black people have dreamed of returning home. At the end of the 18th century, Blacks from Britain, Nova Scotia and Jamaica settled in Sierra Leone. In the 1920s, Marcus Garvey organized the Black Star Line to carry black people back. In 1959, thousands of Jamaicans bought tickets to Africa and jammed the docks of Kingstown waiting for boats that never showed up. At the end of the 20th century, Oba is in regular contact with Rastas living in Africa and is himself sure that he will reach those shores.

So it was that in their meeting with the Prime Minister, Rastas raised the issue of repatriation and were assured by Gonsalves that he would write the government of Ethiopia and initiate a discussion of issues related to travel, cultural exchanges, and the possibility of free access to Ethiopia for the Rastas of St. Vincent.

The Nyahbinghi are also pursuing reparations to provide travel and resettlement assistance to those descendents of Africa who wish to return. Oba says, "Not everyone will want to go but for those who do, they should be assisted by those responsible for the slave trade. Garvey didn't expect everyone to go to Africa and we're not begging for anything. It's a justice situation. Just like the Jews who got money from Germany for what happened to them. . . ."

"Dafina and I definitely see that move as an important part of our future. We have a brother who comes and goes there now and others just want to go and stay. The fact is that our experience in St. Vincent has not been a good one. We haven't been treated very well, you know. We feel we'll have a more free development process in Africa and that we're part of the renewing process of Africa's ancient culture and glory. There's no Rasta who's gone to Africa who's not been rejuvenated. It's an overwhelming experience. There's nothing more important to the Nyahbinghi than getting to Africa."

The Rasta women had similar thoughts. I Deka stressed that "we have to repatriate our minds before we make it physically but yes, I Man I and I see ourselves in Africa. The timing is up to the Father and not for us to predict."

I Land would love to live in Africa "but first you have to prepare your mind."

Azizza Miyazya agreed with her sisters and added, "Africa is a vast place and it happen that his majesty designate Shashamane as a place for people from the west. We see a crisis happening . . . a worldwide crisis. We're talking about Biblical prophecies of disasters. It's not that we don't want to stay in SVG or America but the time is at hand that we have to make a decision and have to repatriate because we have no other choice. His Majesty saw it as something his people will need to do because we're talking about catastrophe breaking out, we're talking about tidal waves. If a volcanic eruption takes place at Kick'em Jenny (an underwater volcano between St. Vincent and Grenada) what happen to St. Vincent? We know it doesn't exist no more because the Almighty is going to come to strike the wicked, they are creating chaos on his earth and they're not going to be allowed to destroy his creation."

2003 Nyahbinghi Gathering in Jamaica

Oba's thoughts in the spring of 2003 returned repeatedly to a mighty gathering of Nyahbinghi from all over the Caribbean to be held during the summer in Jamaica. He hopes he and others from St. Vincent can be there to gain from the strength of thousands of assembled Rastafarians and to take part in the selection of a new body of elders to guide the worldwide movement.

Interactions with Rastas from across the Caribbean might also have an unsettling effect on the Rastas of St. Vincent because Rasta men and women who have moved freely on international circuits for years have often been influenced by a range of ideas not commonly shared by the Nyahbinghi of the smaller islands. Oba was clearly influenced by the various social currents he encountered in the United States and returned to St. Vincent with, for example, commitments to the equality of women not shared by many other Rastas in the 1970s.

It is fairly easy to reject objections to Rasta practices and convictions when they're offered by people outside the movement. It is harder to ignore challenges when they're proposed by those who have been leading and respected Rastafarians for decades. As Oba puts it, "There are Rastas moving around the international scene with laptops now and they're setting the trend even though there's lots of resistance."

For example, when Oba was "sealed up in the faith" at a Nyahbinghi gathering in Jamaica during he 1980s, the well known and popular Rasta poet Mutabaruka was one of the "notables" in attendance. It is quite likely that he will be present at the 2003 Nyahbinghi which Oba so enthusiastically anticipates. Today, Mutabaruka, a man who travels widely and regularly, is encouraging Rastas not to limit their thoughts and traditions to what is found in the Bible because Ethiopian and African wisdom existed long before the Bible was written and should therefore be taken into account.

"When Rastafarians began the quest to find Self," he writes on his website, "the only book that was available to us was the Bible and so the totality of what we understood to be true was based primarily on the interpretation of this book. Even the idea of Haile Selassie as an Afrikan God was justified and validated by the Bible. We, as Afrikan people brought here from Afrika under inhumane conditions, were forced to live—even now—without any kind of identity. This was also justified through the Bible by the European invaders and those Afrikans who sought to rationalize this enslavement by declaring that this was an Act of God. The influence of this book runs deep. Over the years, Rastafarians declared themselves to be Israelites as referred to in the Old Testament, so that words and phrases such as Zion, Promised Land, the wicked Pharaoh and Jah became part of the language of the Rastafarian movement.

"What I am really trying to say here, is that our own religious knowledge goes back no further than the . . . history presented by this Bible. . . . History and archeological evidence prove Ethiopia and Egypt existed thousands of years beyond that. . . ."

Mutabaruka here opens the door to an entirely new set of African traditions that Rastas might claim as their own if they followed his lead and opened themselves to an African perspective broader than that contained in the Old and New Testaments.

One example of the dramatic impact such an opening already represents in some Rasta circles is this interpretation of the Old Testament and patriarchy offered by "Rootswoman" on the web site of "Rastafari Speaks."

"The Hebrews were a nomadic patriarchal tribe of sheepherders and warriors who invaded land long belonging to the matriarchal Canaanites. There they established themselves on Canaanite land with their sky and thunder god Yahweh, calling themselves his 'chosen people.' Yahweh's male prophets and priests had to carry on a continuous struggle against their own people from worshipping the Goddess of the Eastern people. This constant fight against the matriarchal religion and customs is the primary theme of the Old Testament."

"The very first thing that the Levite writers did, as an act against the women, was to have her and her symbols cursed in the garden. The old Goddess religion was damned, her people slaughtered and the stolen mythology of the new male god was written down by male, so called prophets and thus given textual authority as the word of God."

A Rasta Family

The children of Dafina and Oba are the first in their families to be born of Rasta parents. Oba was in his twenties and Dafina in her teens before either knew much about Rastafari. Their children, however, received their first, warm impressions of

Rastas in Dafina's arms. The children's names are African and distinct: Tesfa, Myra, Itara, Askalae, Kaylah, and Siyanda. Their locks, their food, the clothes they wear are different and mark them off in the neighborhood and school. And the word that follows them when old enough to explore beyond the house is always, "We're Rasta, don't forget that."

Ask Dafina how she and Oba are teaching their children to be Rastas and she says, "By living it with them, not by talking about it." A photograph of Selassie is on the wall, Bob Marley's music is on the player, and the children go with them to Rasta communal and public events. When Prince Ermias visited St. Vincent, Oba, Dafina and the children were there. Day after day, Dafina has been with them: working in the house, walking the road to the store, listening, encouraging, straightening things out. When Oba was working on the "Frontline of Liberation Square," one of the children was often at his side.

The locks, the diet, and the clothing help them remember that their family goes a different way but the way cannot, should not be forced. "Rastas don't put force on anyone to change," Dafina says. "We don't go door to door preaching and pleading and chanting people down. We want people to be free."

The main problem Rastas have raising Rasta children is, Oba believes, that Rastas don't have their own institutions. "Our children are still accessing the institutions of Babylon which we deplore. There's never been a full acceptance of Rasta children in the public schools. We don't go with vaccinations but the children are forced to take them. When it's Ash Wednesday, the schools take all the children to a church. If we were in Ethiopia, it'd be different. We'd all be together."

It hasn't been easy. Oba and Dafina returned from the States in 1991 and lived in a good house inherited by Oba and his sister from their mother. They had enough money to buy a boat and get a new life started but the money disappeared, slipped away on loans that never got repaid, generous gifts to friends and allies. They lost the boat and the income earned by carrying supplies. Oba took on odd jobs, sold merchandise throughout the island, T-shirts in the Grenadines, unloaded barrels on the docks at Christmas time. He got his license as a tour guide and made a little here and there, planted a garden for food and sales. It wasn't enough. The electricity was cut off; they couldn't afford to repair the house or fix the roof. In the rainy season, the house was flooded. Some mornings the only breakfast for the children came from the mango tree.

As the children grew, so did concerns about their education. They began to think seriously about moving back to the States. But how do you move a family when there's no money? The way was opened in the summer of 2002 when Dafina visited her family in New York City and learned that she was pregnant with her sixth child. She decided the time had come, decided to give birth in the States and to move her children north. And somehow she made it happen. Early in 2003, Itara, Askalae, and Kaylah joined Dafina and Siyanda, the newborn, in Vermont where they were living with a close friend. Oba and the two older children, Tesfa and Myra, flew north later in the year.

Oba intends to continue his work with the Nyahbinghi of St. Vincent. He wants to work a full season on a Vermont organic farm so he can return to St. Vincent with the knowledge and supplies needed for similar production there, production that might serve as a model for what an agro-army of young people might accomplish on the island of his birth.

The year 2003 has been marked by dramatic changes in their family life. Though the future cannot be known, certain convictions and hopes remain secure. They want, most of all, "to live free," free of Babylon and the consumer culture that drives people harder and faster to buy more and more, a system that funnels the enormous wealth of the world into the hands of a celebrated few and "turns the poor empty away." They do not believe they can transform Babylon. Babylon will be destroyed in the Almighty's way and time but in the "mean" time of these times, they will try to live righteously and fashion a family in which six young children may grow to feel strong about themselves and generous toward others, committed as Rastas to a world in which the poor and vulnerable are treated with the respect and care too long denied.

Notes

1. Eric Hobsbawm, *Age of Extremes* (Vintage, 1996), 218.
2. David Levering Lewis, *W.E.B. Dubois* (Henry Holt, NY, 1999), xv.
3. Cecil Ryan and Cecil Blazer Williams, *From Charles to Williams, Part One* (Projects Promotion Ltd.), 24.
4. James Ferguson, *Eastern Caribbean* (Latin America Bureau, 1977), 57–58.
5. Barry Chevannes, *Rastafari Roots and Ideology* (Syracuse University Press, 2000), 91.
6. W. F. Elkins in *Garvey, Africa, Europe, the Americas*, ed. Rupert Lewis and Maureen Warner Lewis (UWI, Jamaica, 1986), 40–41.
7. Leonard Barrett, *The Rastafarians* (Beacon Press, 1997), 78.
8. Edgar Adams, *Linking the Golden Anchor with the Silver Chain* (St. Vincent, 1996), 9.
9. Mario Moorhead, *Who Feels It Knows It* (copyright 1994 by Mario Moorhead), 10.
10. Campbell, *Rasta and Resistance* (African World Press, 1987), 35–36.
11. Frank Jan Van Dijk in *Chanting Down Babylon* ed. Murrell, Spencer, McFarlane (Ian Randle Publishers, 1998),186.
12. Campbell, 158.
13. Ana Castillo, *Massacre of the Dreamers* (Penguin, 1995), 123.
14. Maureen Rowe, "Gender and Family Relations in Rastafari" in *Chanting Down Babylon*, 72.
15. Campbell, 162–163.

16. Ibid., 163–166.
17. James Ferguson, *Grenada, Revolution in Reverse* (Latin American Books, 1990), 117–118.
18. Imani Tafari-Ama, "Rastawoman as Rebel" in *Chanting Down Babylon*, 95.
19. Ferguson, *Grenada, Revolution in Reverse*, 117–118.
20. Tim Hector website, *Fan the Flame*, June 2, 2000.
21. Barrett, *The Rastafarians*, 93.
22. Ibid., 148–149.
23. Ralph Gonsalves, *The Politics of Our Caribbean Civilization* (Great Works Depot, 2001), 208–209.
24. Edgar Adams, *Linking the Golden Anchor with the Silver Chain* (Edgar Adams, 1996), 70–72.
25. Gonsalves, 309.
26. Ibid., 15.
27. G.A. Griffin, "Murder on the Green," *Transition,* 74, p. 12–13.
28. Leonard Barrett, *The Rastafarians*, 104.
29. Rex Nettleford, "Discourse on Rastafarian Reality, in *Chanting Down Babylon,* 311.
30. Maureen Rowe, "Gender and Family Relations in Rastafari" in *Chanting Down Babylon*, 75.
31. Imani M. Tafari-Ama, "Rastawoman as Rebel" in *Chanting Down Babylon*, 92,104.

Glossary

Rastafarian: A follower of Ras Tafari, a royal title referring to Haile Selassie who was crowned Emperor of Ethiopia in 1930.

Babylon: An ancient city of Mesopotamia located on the Euphrates River about 55 miles south of present day Baghdad to which Jews were taken in the 6th century BC and held captive. Rastas consider themselves captive in the rotten Babylon of the present age and anticipate their liberation by Jah Rastafari Selassie I.

Nyahbinghi: A term derived from an African anti-oppressor movement which now refers to an important assembly open to all Rastas or, more specifically, to the Nyahbinghi Order of Rastas contrasted with other orders such as the Twelve Tribes or the Bobo Dread.

Duppy: Ghostlike creatures, possibly harmful, who come out at night in cemeteries and dark spaces.

Natty Dread: A term made popular by Bob Marley which refers to the Rasta's uncombed, "knotty" hair, the "dreads" which began to be used in the 1940s.

Kaunda: Kenneth Kaunda led Zambia to independence in 1964 and served as the country's President until 1991.

Marcus Garvey (1887–1940): Jamaican organizer and Pan-African leader of the United Negro Improvement Association.

Advocate of Black independence, self-reliance, and movement "Back to Africa."

Ho Chi Minh (1890–1969): A founder of the IndoChina Communist Party in1930 who led the struggle against French colonizers and organized the National Liberation Front (Vietcong) to fight against the USA-supported South Vietnam regime. President of the Democratic Republic of Vietnam (North Vietnam) 1945–1969.

Ernesto "Che" Guevara (1928–1967): Physic[illegible] born in Argentina who joined Fidel Castro to fight for th[illegible]row of Fulgencio Batista's regime in C[illegible] Kille[illegible]